Praise for *The Self-Care Mindset*

"This is a generous and profound book, a book worth sharing. It will stick with you for years to come."
—Seth Godin, Author, *The Practice*

"When you change your relationship with work, everything changes. And Jeanette Bronée's brilliant book shows you how, regardless of your starting point. A must read for every individual and organization aspiring to live well and to work well."
—Karen Mangia, *Wall Street Journal* Best-Selling Author and Salesforce Executive

"*The Self-Care Mindset* is a wonderful contribution to our world at this crucial moment in time. Jeanette gives us the tools to cut through the noise and reclaim agency over the drama in our minds that is burning many of us out."
—Cy Wakeman, *New York Times* Best-Selling Author of *No Ego* and *Life's Messy, Live Happy*

"If you, like me, grew up believing you could be anything you want to be, only to find yourself exhausted and burning out by the constant pursuit of the goals that have come to define you, then this book is a must-read. Jeanette gives us the much-needed tools to rethink what it means to use our minds and take a step at a time toward excellence, while showing us how to listen for the small clues inside each of us that ask us to care for our mental health along the way."
—Steve Burn, Emmy-Nominated Actor, Original Host of *Blue Clues*

"A pathway to healing and transformation, *The Self-Care Mindset* is a must for anyone who cares about how they show up in life. Jeanette Bronée provides the kind of inquiry we all need and a shift toward the performance we all want."
—Chris Westfall, *Forbes* contributor and author of *Easier, Leadership Language* and *The NEW Elevator Pitch*

"This is a book that will change your mind about emotional well-being at work. Jeanette gives us the tools to change the conversation about self-care so that we can unlock our greatness within."

—Claude Silver, Chief Heart Officer, VaynerMedia, Keynote Speaker

"Jeanette Bronée—my friend, student, and teacher—in her new book, *The Self-Care Mindset,* is asking all the right questions. Her framing of the pervasive self-care paradigm is refreshing and potent. At the same time, rather than offering new age platitudes, she is proposing some simple and direct perspectives and actions that any of us can implement to upgrade our state of mind and act efficiently and with impact in the real world."

—David Nichtern, Founder/CEO Dharma Moon, Author of *Creativity, Spirituality & Making a Buck*

"I have always admired how Jeanette can make the concept of self-care so tangible and approachable. Many of us, myself included, struggle with burnout. We push ourselves so hard either because of the expectations we feel from others, or the ones we put on ourselves. *The Self-Care Mindset* will give you all of the frameworks, questions, and tools you need to manage that invisible struggle. Jeanette presents all of it with depth, practicality, and compassion. As we seek to de-stigmatize mental health struggles, learn to navigate an increasingly stressful world, and cultivate kind and safe workplaces, *The Self-Care Mindset* should be on all of our bookshelves, but especially for those in leadership positions."

—Jeff Gibbard, Author of *The Lovable Leader: Build Great Teams with Trust, Respect, and Kindness*

"Working over 20 years in the tech industry and 10 years as a leader at Google showed me that companies reward one behavior above all others: consistent peak performance. How do we achieve it without burning out and giving up on our family, friends, and our health? *The Self-Care Mindset* is a highly original book that provides the questions and accessible tools to allow us to do just that. It gives us the strategies to harness our strength, heart, and mindset to thrive in the modern workplace while protecting our most important resource: our humanity."

—**Jorge Giraldo, Founder and Head Coach of**
Genminds.co, **Former Google Executive.**

The
SELF-CARE
MINDSET

RETHINKING HOW
WE CHANGE *and* GROW,
HARNESS WELL-BEING, *and*
RECLAIM WORK-LIFE QUALITY

The
SELF-CARE
MINDSET

JEANETTE BRONÉE

WILEY

For general information on our other products and services or for technical support, please contact our Customer Care Department within the United States at (800) 762-2974, outside the United States at (317) 572-3993 or fax (317) 572-4002.

If you believe you've found a mistake in this book, please bring it to our attention by emailing our reader support team at wileysupport@wiley.com with the subject line "Possible Book Errata Submission."

Wiley also publishes its books in a variety of electronic formats. Some content that appears in print may not be available in electronic formats. For more information about Wiley products, visit our web site at **www.wiley.com**.

Library of Congress Cataloging-in-Publication Data is Available:

ISBN 9781119986850 (Cloth)
ISBN 9781119986881 (ePub)
ISBN 9781119986898 (ePDF)

Cover Image and Design: Wiley
Author Photography: Torkil Stavdal
Graphics: Jenny L Miles

SKY10036135_092722

To my mom, who taught me that mental health is about listening to the heart.
To my dad, who taught me that curiosity is the fuel of life and leadership is listening with the heart.

Contents

Acknowledgments

How do I thank everyone who has been part of getting me to the point of having created *The Self-Care Mindset*®? This book is a collection of life experiences and people I have met along the way. It's here because of teachers and mentors who have guided me. It's here because of people who have supported me and people who have not. People who have inspired me, some by believing in me, some who don't even know that they have. We learn and grow from all of it. This book is the cause and effect of every decision and choice I have ever made and every person who has been part of my life—some in small ways, some in big moments. Thank you for being a part of a journey that keeps evolving. I continue to learn and remain curious; it is a promise I have made to myself, but I cannot accomplish it on my own. This can only be done with people who are willing to show up and care.

However, this book would not be what it is without my absolutely awesome writing coach and editor, Michael Thompson, who told me there's no way we can write a good book in 72 days, and then accepted the challenge. He went through his own life's curveballs and didn't abandon me in the midst of it. He also got his own book deal while helping me write mine, and he stayed on. Thank you for helping me make a good book, Michael. I'm proud of the work we did, and I appreciate that you let me use the tools I teach, when we might have gotten stuck in the FUD of being able to make this happen. And thank you for accepting my sometimes messy thoughts, too many ideas, and giving me your honest feedback so that we made sense of everything I wanted to share here on these pages. Thank you to Stephen Moore for jumping on board and catching up to help us get to the finish line on time.

Thank you to Rochelle Rice, who is always my feedbacker when I need to process my fears and my thoughts. Thank you to Chelsea and Taylor, who would cook dinner when I was tired from traveling, speaking, and writing all at the same time, and who would listen to me and share the hope that we can change work. Your enthusiasm helped me focus on what I care about and why this book matters. Thank you to my spiritual teacher, Peter Levie, who kept reminding me to open my heart while writing to let more of me come through. Thank you to Diane April, who came to take care of me after my skin-cancer surgery. I was able to recover with ease and get back to writing the book, reminding me that life-long friends continue to show up with the one potion that heals you faster—love. Thank you to Michael and Amy Port who have been part of the two major transitions in my life and have given me tools to reinvent myself, which in 2016 culminated in becoming a TEDx and global keynote speaker. Thank you to Torkil Stavdal for his masterful photography, always making me shine and, without fail, stepping up to take care of Maya when I need to be on the road. Thank you to Ferrazz, who has cut my hair for more than 30 years and even travels on his motorcycle with scissors in his backpack because I'm in town for just a day and also showed up the day my dad died to help me out.

Thank you to everyone who has ever said, "You can ask me for help." And thank you to friends who have called me while writing this book to tell me how awesome they think it is that I get to share my work, which has grown so much over the past 18 years into being able to share it with you. It's a privilege that I have so much gratitude for. Thank you to clients who have trusted me to guide and coach them through the years. Thank you to the companies that hire me to help them change their culture because it matters for our shared future.

And lastly, thank you to Brian Neill from Wiley who contacted me and said, there's a book missing in this world, and I think you are the one to write it.

Life is a reminder that a book is for the people who read it, not the person who writes it. Essentially this is not my book, it's your book, and I hope it will be like a friend on your journey.

Thank you for caring and sharing.

Introduction

"Being human is not a problem to solve; it's an advantage to harness."

It happened at 10 a.m. on a Tuesday. As always, I was at work. I called my mom to ask what time my dad's flight would arrive from Denmark. He was returning to NYC where he was staying with me to continue his chemo treatment for bladder cancer at Memorial Sloan Kettering. My mom had decided to stay behind in Denmark after having just gone through radiation for her third bout with breast cancer. Yes, you read that correctly—both my parents were battling cancer at the same time in two different countries.

That morning, she could barely speak. I asked her what was wrong, and she said she couldn't breathe and was on her way to the hospital. It all happened so fast. I told her to hurry. When the call came an hour later, notifying me that she had died in the ambulance at 11:05 a.m., I finished my work, told my team I'd be gone for a few days and went home to prepare to tell my dad about her passing.

I can still remember waiting for my dad to arrive at my apartment. It was the hardest day of my life. My mom had died only a few hours earlier, and with no time to process it, all I could think of was how I was going to tell my dad that she had died alone while he was on a plane.

No matter what I did, I couldn't fix the pain. No matter what I did, I couldn't ignore it either.

The only thing I *could* do was sit there and wait for him to arrive. And all we could do was cry together once I was finally able to tell him. I didn't get to say goodbye to my mom. I wish in that moment I had told her I loved her but we didn't say those words to each other. Our relationship had always been difficult

1

and remained so even though I was now an adult. As for my dad, he told me they had fought before he left for the airport so he hadn't said a proper good-bye either.

Had I known then what I know now, I would have paused and taken time away from my fast-paced fashion executive job when my mom asked me to meet for lunch or go Christmas shopping with her. I would have taken time off to go back to Denmark and be with her during her treatment. I would have said no to being available 24/7 for business phone calls during dinner with my parents. I would have thanked my mom for ensuring my home was taken care of while I was at work and the two of them awaited their next treatment cycle.

I would have.

I could have.

I should have.

We Don't Have to Accept the Way Things Are

Throughout our early years, we gather beliefs about who we are and what is expected of us while telling ourselves many stories to try to navigate our lives. The problem is that until much later in life, rather than question these beliefs and stories we are told, we tend to accept them as the way things are and the way we should be.

Early on I was trained to believe that my emotions were an inconvenience and it was best to keep my feelings and tears to myself. It ran in the family. My grandfather, a big, burly man who had little time for emotions, was a butcher in Denmark. My great-grandfather was similar to my grandfather, except he was a blacksmith. Growing up, they were my image of what it meant to be resilient. And little me believed that to get through life, I had to be tough like them.

I felt isolated as a kid and was bullied at school. It made me an angry teenager who acted tough to show I didn't care what other people thought about me. Family life was equally disconnected, including several suicide attempts by my mother when I was a teenager, which she would sometimes blame on me for not being a nice and caring daughter. She was bipolar but refused treatment because she thought that meant she would be considered insane. As a teenager, I felt responsible for her moods and behavior and as I progressed into adulthood, I continued to put up a front to ignore the impact of her mental illness. I was what I thought it meant to be tough and resilient, at home, in life, and at work.

Like so many people, my reality was that I had a lot of ideas about what my life "should" be like and who I was "supposed" to be. I adopted different personalities for the simple fact that I wanted to be someone I wasn't and I was hiding my sensitive side. This mindset stuck as I advanced in my career. I worked 24/7 and pushed through challenges by sucking it up and keeping my emotions under wraps to reach my professional goals and what I thought my peers expected of me. The closest I got to any resemblance of "self-care" was taking a little time for lunch, which meant eating at my desk while working and downing coffee to stay awake and energized enough to feel an ounce of motivation.

Unfortunately, I'm not alone in feeling or acting this way. Society has taught us that we have to be focused and resilient to perform at our best. We can't waste time on things that are not related to work, and we believe that expressing our emotions means being overly sensitive, which is often viewed as a weakness. We think showing emotion is opening ourselves to being vulnerable, leaving us open to attacks, and at times, being shamed or leaving us feeling ashamed for having emotions in the first place.

For me though, accepting the way things are—or at least how I envisioned them in my head—came to a full stop the day my mom died, and my father received a terminal diagnosis the same year.

The Painful Wake-Up Call

My dad and I sat together at the doctor's office as we were told that there was nothing left they could do for his cancer and that he only had a few weeks to live. My journey of self-care and definition of what it means to be resilient changed forever over the months that I was the caregiver for my dad as he approached the end of his life. Our conversations transformed me. They were a gift. It was the most difficult and also the most beautiful time of my life. I learned how to be vulnerable and talk about my emotions in a whole new way. We both did. We reminisced about our good times and our most cherished memories while also talking about our past intentions and how we interpreted each other's actions. For example, for 40 years, I never thought we'd actually hugged before and physically embraced in a loving way. I viewed him patting my shoulders when we hugged as him telling me that enough was enough, when in reality, he was trying to convey I was enough and he loved me.

Prior to these conversations, I thought resilience was to ignore my feelings. But this time with my dad opened my eyes to the power of using my feelings as information to cultivate connection and communicate in a way that allowed me not only to understand myself better, but also others. For those five months, we talked about life choices, work, ambitions, goals, regrets, what we care about, what matters in the end, and what it means to love.

As a result, I started asking myself a lot of questions; questions my dad had taught me to ask that allowed for more curiosity, clarity, and courage to emerge. He always told me that the most important skill in life is to learn to listen, truly listen. This is especially true when listening to what we don't say because that's how we start to listen with our heart. I really love this message, and I began practicing it after my parents' deaths. It has changed my life.

I wanted to be of service and I wanted to do work that matters to both me and to others. During this process, for the first time in my life I really dug into myself by asking questions like:

- "How do I want to spend my days?"

- "What would work-life quality look like for me?"

- "What is something I would love doing for years to come?"

- "What would I look back on and be proud to have done or achieved?"

- "What would I do even if I wasn't paid for it?"

- "How do I live a rich life, not abundant in money, but in meaningful relationships, starting with the one I have with myself?"

I realized that always learning and growing was important to me. I loved change and solving problems. My eyes also opened to how much I cared about health, especially mental health because of how my mom's struggle with bipolar disorder had affected my life. Lastly, I wanted work to be an important part of my life. I began to make different choices. I left my job as a burned-out fashion executive, and I went back to school to learn how to help people be healthy *and* busy at the same time because I think we deserve to have it all.

Two decades have passed since I made that decision. Since that time, my work rethinking self-care at work has taken me into countless boardrooms and family rooms across the globe. I've given talks on the subject on hundreds of stages and worked one-on-one with thousands of coaching clients from CEOs of multinationals to entrepreneurs and start-ups to help them reclaim agency over their lives.

As I turn 60 this year, I still ask a lot of myself. I keep using my own tools to stay curious and to keep learning what I need so that I can keep growing and be at my best as I age. I often thank my body for being good to me as we've become a good team and thoughtful of each other. Minus a few wrinkles and back kinks, today I feel better than I did in my 30s when I was fighting against myself to work harder. I'm no longer willing to choose between my career, my friends, and my health. I want it all. And I need self-care for that. We all do.

But in order for self-care to work better for us, we need to unlearn, rethink, and redefine self-care in our new and constantly changing world.

Rethinking Self-Care

Before we dive in, I want to be clear that this is not a book of answers, but rather a book of questions. We each need to uncover and define what works best for us on our individual journeys and there are already mountains of self-help books and prescriptions for self-care. But as burnout rates continue to escalate, it's clear they aren't working for us. At least not for very long, as the moment life gets tough, instead of caring for ourselves, we prioritize work and then rinse and repeat with each new challenge we meet.

Most people think that we just need to know what to do and then we will do it. In my experience, that's not how it works. If we don't come to the answer ourselves, we resist. If we are honest about it, we hate being told what to do, don't we? That's human nature and there's nothing wrong with you for struggling with that.

I always say self-care is a relationship we have with ourselves, and for that relationship to be a healthy one, we need to have healthy conversations with ourselves. We need to be curious and kind, and we need to learn to listen better before we respond. After all, being human isn't a problem to solve, it's an advantage to harness.

Think, Engage, Act

We have three core relationships: the one we have with ourselves, the one we have with others, and the one we have with work, which all overlap with our physical, emotional, and mental well-being. In the pages that follow, we are going to explore how these three core aspects of self and our lives interconnect as how we think, engage, and act. The key is that we learn to connect and communicate better with ourselves and each other to ultimately collaborate better by having the tools to be whole humans at work, at home, and on the go.

It is time we stop thinking of ourselves as not good enough, not doing enough, and that we are a problem to solve. Let's take reality by the horns and instead create a better work-life quality so that we can be who we are meant to be.

To kick things off, in Part I we will challenge the way we THINK about self-care. We will explore what we believe about self-care and how it might be what gets in the way of us actually "doing" self-care. We will also explore how the body and mind work under stress and what we need to rethink the way we function to better harness our human advantage. We will be introduced to a tool I developed called Power-Pausing, which we will be turning to throughout the book as it's the foundation for helping us reclaim agency to connect, communicate, and collaborate better with ourselves and others.

In Part II we move into the ENGAGE aspect of the book. This is where we learn the CARE framework, which consists of self-communication, self-awareness, self-responsibility, and self-expression. I have developed this framework over the years of working with people one-on-one using different tools that I learned partly through studying and getting certified in using different modalities and partly through learning how to overcome challenges in my own life. We will also explore how to cultivate tools to navigate the realities of stress and face the FUD (fear, uncertainty, and doubt) in the workplace to not just get through life feeling less beat up by it, but rather learning how to use it in a productive care-driven way.

We have to stop waiting for things to change and instead change how we deal with *what is* to create the change we want to see.

That's what Part III, ACT, is about. We will pull together the learnings from the previous two parts to harness our choices, behaviors, and actions. We will dig into another framework I developed called AAA (Acknowledge, Accept, Ask) to build our resilience and learn tools to make better and faster decisions to truly harness what it means to be a whole human at work. You will see how everything is interconnected and everything is a relationship and how the key to our well-being is to make all our relationships work better for us.

The future of work demands something different from us. And let's face it, we want something different from the future of work too. Instead of being a place that burns us out, what if work was a place that feeds, fuels, helps us grow, and live better lives?

Learning how to use The Self-Care Mindset® is about both personal and professional growth. The tools will help you continue to change, grow, and evolve your relationship with work without losing your *self* and health. It's the key that unlocks your human advantage so you can let work and life merge in a healthy, productive, and constructive way.

PART I

Think—Rethinking Self-Care at Work

CHAPTER 1

What If We Have Self-Care All Wrong?

"Self-care is not something we do after work to recover; it's how we work better all day long so we don't have to recover."

In 2019, the self-care industry surpassed $10 billion in revenue and is still growing steadily. Since the COVID-19 pandemic, online searches for self-care-related topics and products have increased by 250 percent. The market is booming and apps, hacks, snacks, creams, bath salts, diets, juices and a mountain of other products and services entice people looking for help. Most of us are looking for answers to help us survive our lives a little better, avoid the burnout and exhaustion we feel, or discover diet options to lose the COVID-15 we put on during lockdown. As conversations about mental health have increased, there's been a rallying cry to care for our physical, emotional, and mental well-being.

But it's not working, is it?

Instead, we have an entire population feeling burned out, frazzled, and thinking spa treatments, bubble baths, and aromatic candles will somehow make our problems go away. Prior to COVID, we were already experiencing a public health epidemic. We have to ask if taking time off to pamper ourselves to recover from work is really sustainable and how we really want to live. After all, many of us feel like nothing has changed after taking a few days off; within a day or two of returning to work, our vacation often feels like a distant memory.

It took me two burnouts and losing both of my parents within a year to cancer before I realized that self-care is a daily mindset, not something we do only on weekends to recover from a stressful week. Socrates introduced us to self-care in ancient Greece as knowing ourselves so that caring for ourselves is how we can care for loved ones. The sense that self-care is not just about us has been part of the human condition since we appeared on earth. Buddhism speaks about compassion for ourselves so that we can have compassion for others. We are all interconnected.

Self-care is not just about self. It's about care.

When searching for self-care online, millions of results come up. If you look for the official definition, we see self-care mentioned in relation to healthcare, and as such, it's no longer preventive but rather sick care. Baths didn't cure my worries or ease the pain of losing my parents. Lighting candles never helped me forget looming deadlines either. Does that work for you?

I used to believe being overly stressed at work came with the job and wore it as a badge of honor. I never once questioned sacrificing my personal life to be successful. Nor did I question sacrificing my health to reach my professional goals. Like a lot of people, I accepted that work hurts. But after my parents passed, and I was warned that it was only a matter of time before I'd get cancer too. I decided it was time to reclaim agency over my health, my life, and my career.

Around the globe, we're seeing this played out in real-time with the Great Resignation. People are fed up and tired, and they're leaving their workplaces in droves, thinking a career change is going to fix the problem or to simply rethink what matters most. Sure, money is one factor, but for most, it's because they feel overworked and undervalued. They're burned out and realizing there are more important aspects to life besides a paycheck. They want to reclaim their health and nourish personal relationships every day, not just from time to time. While this crisis seems to be a major issue, it's actually a positive thing that we're talking about it because that means we can do something about it.

Leaving work and reinventing ourselves shouldn't be the solution to preventing burnout and taking back our joy. We have to change the way we work. We have to rethink self-care and what it means to be resilient so we are no longer forced to choose between our health, well-being, relationships, or our careers.

The challenge we face today is not finding work-life balance but cultivating work-life quality. This is why we need to demystify self-care so we no longer have to choose between work and life.

Are Our Beliefs About Self-Care Getting in the Way of Self-Care?

The world has changed, our lives have changed, and in recent years, our work has changed. Despite the disruption, our relationship and understanding of self-care have remained the same.

- We think of self-care as a retreat or something fluffy. But what if instead, we thought self-care was for focused and committed individuals who want to perform consistently at their peak without burning out?

- We think of self-care as a side-hustle—something we do after work to recover. But what if instead, we thought of self-care as how we work better, so we don't have to recover?

- We think of self-care as something we do when we have time. But what if instead, we thought of self-care as giving us time back because we spend it better?

- We think of self-care as a list of perfect habits to do. But what if instead, we thought of self-care as a mindset that helps us better navigate stress?

- We think of self-care as something we do alone. But what if instead, we thought of self-care as the key to building a better and healthier culture?

On and on these paradoxes go. On top of this, we think the cure for burnout is taking time off and our emotions should be hidden or suppressed. But we don't just burn out from working too much, we burn out from worrying too much and our emotions are the last thing we should ignore as they are what defines us as human beings and are the doorway to cultivating connection, communication, and collaboration.

When you look at these paradoxes and misconceptions surrounding self-care and burnout, isn't it clear why self-care isn't working for us? In fact, people think of self-care as a luxury for those with money and time to spare, so no wonder it doesn't help us during stressful events. Or we assume self-care is selfish. In reality, self-care is about asking better questions so that we can know ourselves better, which is something we all need because we are all human beings, and we don't come with a one-size-fits-all manual.

Consider that we haven't rethought how we work since the Industrial Revolution. Back then, people began working feverishly to compete with machines. Not much has changed, has it? We're still trying to keep up with the speed of technology and hack time by abandoning our humanity while leaving behind our self-care the moment we get busy. Even when we're not working, we live in a culture that praises constant activity in our quest to do more, be more, and achieve more.

It's no surprise that we think of self-care as something we do. But it's not something we do. It's who we are. Self-care is not about fixing ourselves; it's about finding our way back home to ourselves.

Rethinking Our Three Core Relationships

We have three core relationships—the one we have with ourselves, the one we have with others, and the one we have with work. Traditionally, we separate these three relationships, juggle them, and do our best to prioritize them. But in our new world, the lines between these relationships have evaporated and are bleeding into each other like never before.

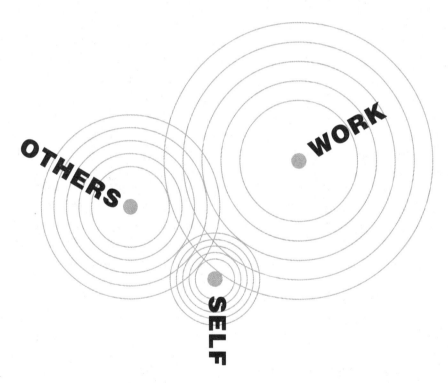

No matter how we spin it, when times get tough, most of us put our work first, personal relationships second, and if we're lucky, lastly, maybe spend some time on ourselves. By continually placing ourselves last though, we won't solve the current burnout crisis. Think about it. While we may like, clap, or leave supportive comments on LinkedIn when someone says, "I'm taking a self-care day," the reality remains that nothing is changing and it certainly won't improve if we keep thinking of self-care as time off.

What's happening here? How did we end up this way? Of course, it's a step forward that we claim time for self-care. But we're still operating from an old mindset about what self-care is and seeing it as an escape from our day-to-day lives to recharge instead of taking charge and treating self-care as the foundation for achieving our goals.

What we need to recognize is that no matter how hard we try to separate ourselves from our tasks and relationships, we are not separate. We—as individuals—are at the core of all our relationships, and this affects all aspects of our interactions in work and life.

Going back to when I was told it was only a matter of time before I got cancer after my parents passed, I knew I had to get in tune with myself. For several years, I had utterly abandoned my self-care in pursuit of a career. So I set out to learn what my body needed so I could challenge the verdict and change my prognosis. I returned to school, learned integrative nutrition therapy, studied different healing modalities, went back to my mindfulness practice, and continued my Buddhist studies. More than anything, I wanted to understand not just what makes us sick, but also how we can reclaim agency over our health.

I need my body to take care of me as much as my body needs me to take care of it. We have an interactive relationship. We need to be a team. You and your body do too.

One pattern I saw emerge in my previous actions came from my Danish culture. I grew up learning that I was weak if I had needs or emotions. Besides learned behavior, I developed a mindset of people-pleasing—always saying yes, never saying no—and constantly being of service while I ignored my own needs. Sometimes it made me feel like a martyr, sometimes the hero, and sometimes just fried because I still didn't feel like I belonged or really mattered at work.

There's a lot of buzz around servant leadership these days, which entails decentralized leadership, encouraging diversity of input, supporting people in growing their self-leadership, and cultivating a culture of trust because people feel they matter. Many people I hear talking about it, though, interpret it as being selfless and doing everything for their people. This viewpoint, however, just leads to burnout and probably not a healthy culture either as opposed to the selflessness that comes from recognizing success is a team effort. When we have the mindset that being of service means doing everything, anytime for others, we are missing the point of what it means to be of service. It's not about who comes first; it is about recognizing how relationships work interactively.

Looking back, I could see how my lack of self-care not only wore me out, but it also affected the people around me, my family and friends, my team, and even my quality of work. I saw how I cut corners to save time, how I had been short-tempered and irritable, impatient, and unkind. This was more evident when I was tired, thirsty, and hangry (hungry and angry), and working in survival mode.

Back then, I had self-care all wrong, and most of us still do because as a society we still have the mindset that to be of service, we must sacrifice ourselves. We must rethink self-care in relation to work so that we no longer have to choose between being busy and healthy or having a career and a life. Fortunately, companies and other workplaces are now realizing they must also take responsibility for their part in changing the narrative so we can survive the future of work and build a better culture together.

Consider this: What could change if your goal is to have a healthy career and a successful personal life? How would you change your perspective and therefore, the way you choose to work and live?

It's time for us to reclaim choice so that we can make self-care at work, work better for us.

Demystifying Self-Care

By now, it's clear that we have to have our basic needs met. Let's stop debating in society whether or not we need fuel and support for our minds and bodies—we do. As we move along in this book, you'll also discover why even our most basic needs are essential to help us manage stress. The important point to remember is that we need to stop thinking of self-care as something we have to do, but rather embrace self-care as who we are and how we care better about ourselves, each other, and our work. After all, a healthy relationship with ourselves affects and cultivates meaningful relationships with others and establishes how we show up for work. The cause and effect of self-care isn't just about looking or feeling better, either. It affects how we think, engage with ourselves and each other, and the decisions we make—and with that—how we live and work as whole human beings.

Left unchecked, we'll continue to take our bodies for granted and ignore the nudges and prompts it gives us throughout the day until something horrific happens, which isn't surprising. We don't grow up learning how amazing our bodies are, and we don't comprehend their self-healing power or that they run entirely in the background all day long to help us function.

Our bodies want us to succeed and are a system that's more complex, intelligent, and faster than any computer. And they don't ask for much. As long as we feed it, give it water, take it for walks, perhaps a run, and make sure it gets some breaks, rest, and sleep, it shows up day after day for us. When you give it some love and care, it works like a loyal companion.

For this to happen, we need to recognize that self-care is both the most intimate and personal relationship we have with ourselves and also the most interesting and amazing possibility we have to harness change and growth and build a better culture together.

But in order to tap into our human advantage, the first thing we need to do is learn to pause more.

CHAPTER 2

Power-Pausing

"Imagine if we would pause more, what could change?"

We live in a culture where we squeeze every minute out of everything we do. We eat while working, drink coffee on the go, answer text messages in meetings, and check email while we're working on different tasks. The demand for our attention is under a constant barrage. Each day we fall further behind schedule with our never-ending to-do lists.

Despite the constant connection, we've become disconnected from ourselves. And even though we have access to all the information we need to feel better, we're just as lost and confused about how to take better care of our minds and bodies, not trusting ourselves to know what we need.

But when's the last time you had a good chat with yourself? I mean a really good chat, a kind and curious one? Where you paused for just a moment and checked in with your body? Your emotions? Mind? Soul? When was the last time you paused and considered what's going on inside and you asked yourself, "How am *I* doing in there?"

My guess is it's been a long time because of the new reality we live in and let's face it, most people have not been taught to do so, ever. If you're like most people, you crave more time for yourself, want to feel less stressed, and be able to handle pressure more effectively. It also doesn't help that we're constantly being encouraged to become healthier, happier, and more successful. Ironically, we have all the information at the tips of our fingers to practice better self-care, achieve our goals, and—dare I say—"Live our best lives!" Yet, somewhere in the midst of this noise and our never-ending pursuit of "the good life," we find ourselves overwhelmed and ill-equipped. Even worse, we might even be hard on ourselves for not taking better care of our mind and body, while simultaneously believing we're failures for not reaching our potential.

So rather than repeatedly beat the same drum and expect a different song, let's explore what we can do to reclaim agency in our lives.

And that begins by learning to *pause, listen, and ask better questions.* I call that "Power-Pausing."

Pause, Listen, Ask

I often hear people say they don't have time to take a break during the day. "*So much to do and so little time!*" Even when I say the word "pause," most people interpret it as a break or "time out." Sure, it could be that. But pausing is also about so much more.

A pause is a brief moment of time where you can exhale to let your nervous system calm down so you can better listen to yourself in order to come back home to yourself. It's giving ourselves the space to listen inside and ask, "How am I in there right now?" A pause can be just a small moment of stillness or a small moment that creates space between thought and action. Instead of continuing to default to reacting, a pause becomes a small window of opportunity where we choose how we want to respond and act.

In short, a pause is that small gap in time where change happens because you can ask: "What do I need right *now* so that I can better face what's in front of me?"

The key that will allow us to unlock how we think, engage, and act with more intent and with less stress is found in how we ask questions. Throughout the rest of this book, we'll talk a lot about "Power-Pausing," and we are going to keep asking ourselves: *"How am I in there right now, and what do I need so that I can. . .?* You will learn to see how this question can be used in any situation that you need to solve for, learning how to pause, listen, and ask yourself over and over again so that you can better face the challenge in front of you to navigate change, harness your self-care, and grow. You can think of it as a mantra that becomes a new way to direct your focus and attention toward what you are working to achieve.

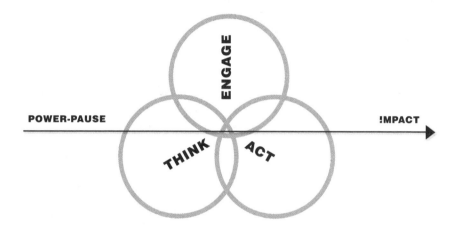

In addition to learning about the relationship we have with ourselves and how pausing makes us more focused, alert, and able to make better decisions, we are also going to use "Power-Pausing" as a tool to interact and engage with others more effectively. Instead of reacting to something, this simple, yet impactful tool gives us that moment of mindfulness—a gap in time—to listen, ask better questions, and make a discerning choice to respond with more care and on purpose.

Your Mind on Pause

The Microsoft Human Factor Lab performed a study where they conducted brain scans to learn what happens to our nervous system when we attend back-to-back meetings as opposed to having short breaks in between meetings.

Their findings are important to take note of.

What researchers discovered is that the brain scans show our mind and nervous system "overheat" when we don't pause and disconnect between meetings or tasks. However, we remain cool-headed when we pause to step away for a moment. In the scans, you can see how stress builds up if we don't take time to pause and release it. Their findings demonstrate that, despite our culture's belief, we cannot be engaged 24/7 or deal with constant input, decision-making, or even pay attention.

YOUR MIND WORKS BETTER
WHEN YOU TAKE BREAKS

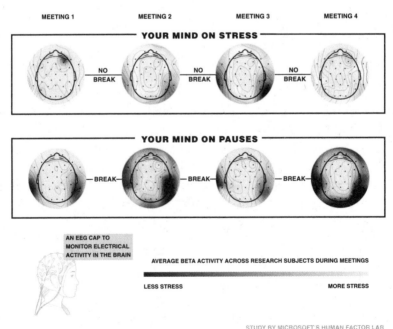

TAKING A PAUSE BETWEEN MEETINGS AND TASKS PREVENTS STRESS FROM BUILDING UP

Source: Path For Life®

No wonder we feel so overwhelmed, right?

Paying attention can feel like stress once we do it for too long. As a quick exercise, think back to a time when you had to focus on the same thing for an extended period. You got tired, didn't you? Or perhaps you felt uncomfortable or irritated?

Studies also show that we focus best for 45–90 minutes at a time. What this teaches us is the need to incorporate moments of disconnection between tasks, meetings, challenges, and engagements.

It'd be easy to close this book and say, "Okay, so I just need to disconnect for five minutes between meetings," but that would miss the point. It's not merely about unplugging, but also connecting, knowing when to plug back in, and what type of support we need. Power-Pausing is a tool we can use to recognize our patterns, understand ourselves better, and reclaim agency in our lives, work, health, and happiness.

Even though it's not taught in our schools or during our upbringings, like any other skill, to pause, listen, and ask questions before we act is a skill we can learn and it's vital to begin the desperate change we need to prevent burnout.

With that said, we're going to practice Power-Pausing. As we begin, take a moment to sit with the following questions to gauge where you are today.

- How much time do you generally spend getting to know yourself, your needs, and your patterns?

- How much time do you think you lose each day because you're exhausted or because your thoughts are elsewhere?

- Why would it matter to you to learn better self-care mindset skills and what kind of change or impact would you like to make?

The Three Types of Power-Pausing

There are three different types of Power-Pausing: the physical pause, the emotional pause, and the mental pause. Each one helps us to reclaim agency over how we think, feel, engage, act, and behave. You can think of it as how we reset our mind and body, re-engage our focus and attention, and reclaim our ability to make better decisions all day long.

1. **The physical pause:** Here we pause to listen to our physical needs in order to reset, recover, and reclaim energy, attention, and focus. This allows us to re-engage and think more clearly.

2. **The emotional pause:** This technique allows us to listen to our emotions to access emotional intelligence (EQ). It's the pause that taps into our limbic brain connected to how we feel. To improve our well-being, we must learn to get in touch with our emotions and use them as information. Power-Pausing helps us reset, listen, and ask what we need to navigate stress and FUD (fear, uncertainty, and doubt). It also helps regulate emotions, like being sad, scared, or mad. This powerful pause creates connection, more empathetic communication, and more effective collaboration with others while helping open up the part of the brain that's curious and able to listen. When we accomplish this, we cultivate belonging. We'll explore this concept more in Part II of the book.

3. **The mental pause:** Here we pause to listen and ask questions that keep exploring what we need to navigate challenges and make better decisions that are inclusive of our self-care. This pause taps into the executive function or the smart brain. We'll dive more into depth on this specific pause in Part III.

POWER PAUSING
THINK, ENGAGE, & ACT WITH CARE

WHAT DO YOU NEED SO THAT YOU CAN?

Each pause is designed to be used in action or to disconnect for a moment. You can do it anywhere and anytime while walking, in a meeting, alone, or when you start a new task or pick up the phone. You can even use it while responding to an email, when you wake up, go to sleep, feel under pressure, or are stuck. Instead of endlessly scrolling or texting while in the bathroom, take a moment and use a Power-Pausing.

If the concept seems strange or vague, think of a pause as meditation where you sit with yourself, observe your thoughts, or simply give yourself space to ask yourself questions and listen before making a choice. It's especially powerful to pause before we react, which is how we reclaim agency over our lives. I'm willing to bet we've all experienced the regret of reacting too quickly or rashly and would love a chance to take our rushed words or actions back.

The First Step of Power-Pausing Is Learning to Breathe Again and Listen to Your Body

For now, we're going to focus on the physical pause and build on it as our foundation as we continue through this book. Five minutes is plenty of time to get the benefits, even if you might want to pause for longer the more you become comfortable using the tool. For now the point is to make the pause meaningful and useful in different scenarios. Here are the instructions. You can read them first and then practice as they're easy to remember:

1. First, start by lowering your gaze or closing your eyes (once you practice more, you'll be able to accomplish this without closing your eyes as lowering your gaze will always be a good way to go inward in the moments when you're not alone).

2. Focus your attention on your breath. Notice if you are breathing solely in your chest, and if so, see if you can breathe all the way down into your belly. Expand your stomach while inhaling—just like you're filling it with air—and then let the breath flow outward without forcing it.

3. After a few deep belly breaths, turn your focus on your exhale and see how that feels. Even just a couple of breaths can be enough of a physical pause to calm your nervous system into a more open and relaxed state as focusing on the exhale helps with anxiety and stress.

4. Stop here for now and notice how your body feels. This is a simple and effective way to center yourself. Let go of the buzzing mind and reconnect with your body as it will help stabilize you.

5. Now take it a step further by observing your feet. See if you're able to "breathe all the way into your feet." Logically, we know

this is impossible, but the intention of drawing energy toward your feet can help you feel calm, centered, and grounded.

6. The last step is to scan your body. Consider how you feel in your legs, back, stomach, chest, neck, shoulders, head, eyes, and throat. All you're doing here is noticing and learning how to pay attention to your body. Please don't judge yourself as you're merely checking to see if you're okay or if you need anything else to feel a smidge better. For example: Are you feeling stiff and achy? Do you feel tired? What about any discomfort? Are you thirsty or hungry? Perhaps you feel fine; it's good to notice that too.

This technique and subsequent pause might be all you need before you begin what's next in your life or on your agenda at work once more. It allows you to manage your stress levels and just *be* for a moment instead of constantly thinking and obsessing so our nervous system can cool off.

The Practice of Pausing on Purpose

Many people hold their breath when stressed. We tense up our muscles and clench our jaw, which stops proper blood circulation to the brain, making us less effective and productive. Power-Pausing, though, teaches us the simple act of breathing again so that we can work in a more relaxed, yet effective state. More accurately stated, we learn to breathe with intent and listen to our bodies from a place of curiosity.

When sitting all day, our body can get stiff. We need to stretch and move. If you're anything like me, you can get impatient when your body isn't comfortable or you've been sitting in the same position for too long.

I start this ritual in the morning before I even get out of bed. With my hands gently resting on my belly, I take a couple of breaths in and focus on the exhale, while scanning my body. This allows me to check in with myself, see how I'm feeling, and ask myself what I need so I can feel at my best as I start my day. I also pause before each meeting to evaluate whether I need to stretch, move, breathe, close my eyes to reset my mindset, get some water, or use the bathroom. I use Power-Pausing as a physical pause between meetings that allows me to regenerate my energy, focus, and attention.

Just a reminder, though: I don't lose those five minutes between meetings by not being productive. Getting my body and mind ready for the next meeting *is* productive because it's how I can give my best rather than feeling achy, distracted, impatient, or moody. After all, no one wants that person in their meeting, am I right?

This is just one example of why we must rethink self-care as how we support ourselves in working better all day so we don't have to recover at the end of it. We owe it to the next meeting that we self-care before we enter.

Building Your Support System

Just like we need scaffolding when building a house, we need a strong foundation when building a healthy career and a successful personal life. Pausing throughout the day to ask ourselves what we need is how we begin to do that as it helps us notice our patterns and needs so we can better support ourselves.

You can start learning:

- How does your energy vary? And when do you need to maintain steady energy or focus?

- What's your attention curve throughout the day?

- When are you best at doing focused work alone, and when are you best at staying present in meetings or when collaborating?

We don't all have the same rhythm, and we don't even all have the same rhythm each day. Using Power-Pausing to check in between meetings, however, is an excellent way to harness self-care to work better for us. And companies are waking up to this also as more and more of them are putting buffers between meetings. But it's up to each of us to ensure we spend that time in a way that truly supports ourselves instead of rushing to check our email.

Practicing the Pause

Everywhere we turn, we're encouraged to go, go, go. If pausing is new to you, give it a shot when you first wake up in the morning. There are many benefits in taking a few minutes as we kick off our day to get aligned with ourselves while asking what we need so that we can better face whatever our day has in store. You can even use the questions of *"Hey, how am I doing in there and what do I need so that I can. . .?"* as a mantra to help you reclaim agency and as a reminder of the power of self-care.

As we move forward, you'll learn why the power of asking questions is such an essential aspect of Power-Pausing and how it helps you manage stress and anxiety by changing your focus and attention.

Remember, we are not fixing ourselves for being broken human beings; we are learning what we need so that we can access our awesome humanity and use it for good. After all, being human is not a problem to solve; it's an advantage to harness.

CHAPTER 3

Unstress to Get Unstuck

"We don't have to become stressed by stressful events."

When I was a fashion executive, I was addicted to coffee. I would start each day with it and schedule meetings based on where I could get the best cup. To say I lived on coffee while teetering on the edge of burnout is an understatement. It was my lifeblood in a fast-paced and toxic work culture. While I liked the designer I worked for, there was an expectation that my life should revolve around work, and large quantities of caffeine helped fuel the lie. Some days, it boosted my ego, because the caffeine high can make you feel powerful, and I told myself that she saw me as superhuman and absolutely crucial to the company. But it also made me accessible every minute of the day because I was constantly anxious from the coffee, and my needs fell to the wayside.

Coffee became my adrenaline crutch. Whether in my hand, on my desk, in the car, or on the subway, you never saw me without it. I grew up in Denmark, where it's customary to sip coffee throughout the day, but I was downing espresso and cappuccino *all day*. It was noticeable enough that even when my parents visited, they asked me if I was okay due to the amount of caffeine I was consuming and the accompanying anxiety level.

Then everything came to a head when both my parents were diagnosed with cancer three months apart, and they came to live with me in the United States.

Despite this, I kept working insane hours, living on coffee, and not facing the reality of my parent's cancer treatments or the impact it had on them. I was high on caffeine to achieve absurd career goals. Coffee highs boosted my focus on accomplishment while I ignored the people closest to me. Isn't it ironic that we paint coffee shops as places to connect, whereas in reality you find people furiously hammering away on keyboards, isolated, and high on fake energy?

Once my mom died unexpectedly—and without me saying good-bye—that became the wakeup call. I hadn't paused to go back to Denmark with her, where she was in treatment, thinking she would recover as she had twice before. She wanted to connect and spend time together, but I was off working and fueling work with my liquid adrenaline crutch. I'm not blaming coffee by any means. But what I realized was that I had built patterns that kept me alienated, stressed out, and in a constant state of emergency, while ignoring the actual emergency in front of me.

I was living and working in survival mode, while missing every essential cue needed for human interaction and basic self-care.

Are You Working and Living in Survival Mode?

Your epiphany doesn't have to be as extreme or dramatic as mine for you to take a moment to pause and reflect on whether you're stuck. You already might hear that nagging voice in the back of your mind whispering that you're operating out of reactive, unhealthy patterns where everything is urgent. Maybe you see aspects of yourself in my story where you put every-thing else on hold: your health, relationships, family, or your personal growth.

When we run on empty and neglect recharging, we end up working in survival mode.

While it may appear that I'm comparing people to machines, remember that the human body needs rest and maintenance, just like mechanical devices to operate fully and not break down. Sure, we want to feel like we have the energy and power of a race car, but more often than not, we never gear up for the big race. Instead, we show up with a run-down hooptie with dents, dings, and engine issues day after day.

Survival mode is an adaptive system that the body enters when experiencing danger or crisis. You've likely heard of it as *fight, flight,* or *freeze*, which is how humans react when faced with a stressful situation.

- We might grow angry seemingly out of nowhere (*fight*).

- We might find ourselves rushing as fast as we can, without thinking about anything other than getting through the situation (*flight*).

- We might feel paralyzed, foggy, overwhelmed, and don't know what to do (*freeze*).

The reality is that we probably feel aspects of all three dur-ing most workdays. Throughout the centuries these are our normal, conditioned human responses. We scan for changes in our environments that signal threat or danger, like being chased by a tiger, or nowadays, the stress of a tight or unreal-istic deadline.

Because our bodies are still part of nature—and our hor-mones and reactions are based on the perception of danger—we adapt. That's great when we have to push through and get something done for the next few hours. The problem is that we now *live* in a constant state of survival mode, and it's wearing us out.

Consider the following: during spurts of survival mode, our digestive system shuts down, body temperature changes, and blood flow goes to the extremities. We might look pale, flushed, or even feel dizzy. The longer we stay in this prolonged state, the more inflammation occurs.

Survival mode is great if we're experiencing an actual threat, but in the modern world, the threat has become *survival stress*, the fear that something may hurt you, causing the body to naturally respond with a burst of energy to allow you to survive the dangerous situation (fight) or escape it all together (flight). It manifests itself as worrying about deadlines, presentations, meetings, tasks, and projects. We use and abuse our bodies' ability to access this hyper-focus to move as fast as possible and crush our workplace fears.

And why do we do it? *Because we can!*

Humans are amazing and resilient. When we need to face down danger, we can run on empty. Survival mode triggers an adrenaline rush that can feel incredible because it gives us the extreme focus and the additional energy we crave. It's why our culture embraces coffee so much, as it's a kick of cortisol in a cup. It's important to keep in mind that cortisol isn't bad, as it's a natural hormone and the hormone that gets us moving, motivated, and focused. We need some cortisol in the mornings to have the necessary energy to get going. It also helps control our metabolism and our immune system.

But more *is not* better. Better is.

As the afternoon rolls around, we actually need less cortisol in order to calm down and prepare for sleep. The thing is, though, that the more we stay in survival mode to get through our day, the higher our cortisol levels stay throughout the day. This then depletes our natural resources and ability to recover. Because the body is a regenerative system, when cortisol is chronically high, inflammation also rises in the body. It's like increased wear and tear with no repair.

Still, cortisol is essential in how we respond to stress and an inter-connected cause and effect. When we feel stressed about a situation, cortisol rises because it's part of our alert system and helps us navigate danger. However, when cortisol remains high, we feel more anxious, stressed, and overwhelmed. This is because spiked cortisol levels affect not only our reflexes and functions but also our mind and how well we can make decisions under stress. This said, even in our day-to-day stress, pressure with work and life, adrenaline rushes, raising cortisol levels, and living on coffee, our stress and anxiety continue to rise to alarming and unhelpful levels.

As an example, do you remember that moment as a kid when you ran so fast that you fell over because your legs couldn't keep up? That's what happens to our mind; it begins to run faster than we do. Our thoughts and nervous system hit overdrive, and our mind gets flooded with cortisol. As a result, instead of feeling like we have things under control, we end up more anxious and stressed.

Long-term overuse of the body's survival mode system and chronically high cortisol levels can cause weight gain, high blood pressure, loss of libido, inflammatory diseases, and mood swings. On the flip side, ending up with cortisol levels that are too low can cause depression, fatigue, muscle weakness, and metabolic issues that can become life-threatening.

If we're honest though, fear of future disease doesn't motivate change right now, because when we are under pressure and stress we only focus on getting through the challenge in front of us.

Essentially, that's the nature of stress and the reason why we tend to abandon self-care even if that's when we need it the most. It's also how we get stuck in the same pattern over and over again because under stress, we want immediate relief and results, which is why we tend to fall prey to excessive food, TV watching, and drinking at night. We let ourselves off the hook, recognize how depleted we are, and we want our mind to stop thinking.

What most people don't realize is that 95 percent of our thoughts and habits are unconscious, while roughly 5 percent we actively engage in. Under stress, we run on that 95 percent, which means we're losing our ability to be curious, creative, and constructive. We fall back on old habits, doing what we've always done, and get stuck on repeat. We can end up in survival mode when we don't drink enough water, eat food, or pause and rest throughout our day. These are our most basic human needs and self-care we abandon when we get busy and we become reliant on much more expensive and fancy recovery options after a long day or work week.

When we don't drink enough water throughout the day, we end up dehydrated. Even if we're only slightly dehydrated, the lack of water can make us feel foggy, forgetful, fatigued, and confused. We can also become irritable, impatient, snappy with our comments, and angry. A prison study some years ago found that when encouraging inmates to drink more water, aggression went down. Sometimes when the elderly start showing symptoms of confusion, weakness, and agitation, they can be mistaken for the onset of dementia, when in reality, they might lack fluids.

You might think, "Come on...it's just water."

I get it. But at the same time, most people I talk to don't drink enough water and believe it or not, one of the leading reasons why is because they don't have time to pee! Adding to that, when we get through the day on coffee and other caffeinated drinks, which are diuretic, we become even more dehydrated.

When we operate this way, our bodies will understand this lack of water, food, or sleep as survival stress. Adding to this, our brain is the organ that consumes the most calories, so when we run low on fuel like glucose that we absorb from food, we end up hangry. I don't know about you, but I'm not pleasant to be around when I'm hangry, and I certainly don't enjoy being in meetings with hangry people.

If you're reading this, I'm sure you want to do good work, build a healthy lifestyle, and be successful as opposed to living in a constant state of duress and stress. However, since we cannot avoid stress in our daily demands as its part of life, let's take a different approach.

Stress Is Like a Pothole

Just prior to my marriage in 1990, I bought a Harley-Davidson motorcycle as a self-expression and identity statement: "I may be tying the knot, but I am still very much my own woman!" While learning to ride, I was constantly warned about the dangers of potholes because you can easily crash if you hit one. I was told, "If you look at the pothole, you're going to hit it, so you have to look in the direction you want to go."

This piece of wisdom applies to many aspects of life because that's how our attention works. Instead of focusing on what we want to avoid, we need to focus on what we want to achieve. Or as I like to say, "Our intention fuels our attention!" If you focus on the path you want to take, the motorcycle follows.

In the same respect, when stressed, we tend to focus automatically on what's not working—the potholes in front of us— rather than pausing to be curious about what we need to make it work. Sure, part of the automatic hijacking of our minds helps us to stay safe when in danger, but when focusing on changes and challenges in front of us we need a different mindset so that we can focus on what's possible.

To find the way forward, we need to pause and ask questions that help us solve for what we are working to achieve and get past the pothole by tapping into what we *care* about, why something matters, what change we want to achieve, and the impact it could have. When doing this, instead of asking ourselves why something is not working, we ask ourselves: "Why does this matter and what do I need so that I can make it work?," which is far more powerful.

I learned the magic of asking better questions from my dad as a child and then later on when I studied hypnotherapy. My training in mindfulness aligned with this process as well and helped me understand how we can tap into the power of the mind simply by pausing and changing the question.

This seemingly simple tool can create tremendous change and impact. When under stress and as our mind becomes hijacked by fear, society has taught many of us to "just ignore" our fears and be brave. However, it's far more powerful to listen to our fear and ask what we need to feel brave. That's a question our mind knows what to do with, and it can help get us out of the pothole when we land in it.

Coaching people for 18 years, I have consistently seen how stress gets us stuck in the inner dialog of what's wrong. Asking what we need so that we can steer toward a solution is how we build a roadmap for ourselves and the scaffolding that supports a healthy life, enjoyable work, and a care-driven culture.

Of course, work and life will never stop causing us stress, but we *can* change how we respond to—and navigate—stress so that it doesn't get us stuck in the pothole, teetering on the edge of burnout.

We Can't Control What Happens, But We Can Control How We Respond

Change is constant in our modern world and something we think we have to be resilient to withstand. However, by Power-Pausing, we learn to be curious and adaptive. It allows us to change and grow without getting stuck in stress and worry, resisting change, and triggering us into working in survival mode to push through.

We often wrongly believe we have to control our environment to avoid or manage stress. But instead, we can improve our ability to navigate stress by pausing and listening to become aware of our stressors and triggers, so that we can make discerning choices about how we can and want to respond. Learning to work more productively with stress is key to reclaiming our health and happiness.

I know all this might sound like a great promise but to harness change, we must recognize that we can't avoid stress unless we decide to leave our jobs. Of course, if your work environment is toxic, this is maybe the best answer. However, even if we do that, it's important to remember that work isn't the only source of our woes and stress. Life is too. What we *can do* is change how we respond to what happens and learn to ask better questions to focus on what we need so that we can get through. When we practice this, we better support ourselves in avoiding life's pot-holes. By focusing on Power-Pausing when stress is hijacking our mind, we create the necessary space between trigger and reaction, which is essential to getting unstuck and moving forward.

Throughout this book, you'll learn how to tap into your exceptional human advantage and use your mind to work better for you by using the tools of The Self-Care Mindset® to harness your innate ability to change and grow.

For now though, I invite you to practice Power-Pausing to get unstressed.

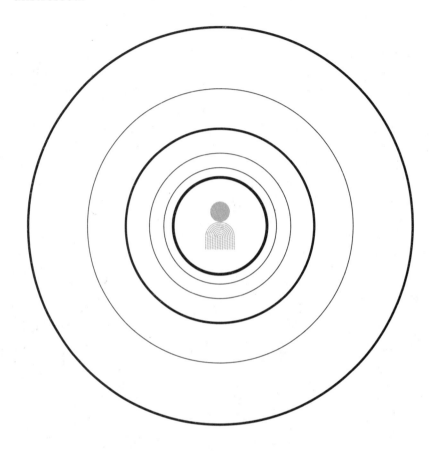

Think of it as a worry-free zone for just a moment. Take a couple of deep breaths into your belly, stretch your body, air out your mind from having to focus, and move your nervous system out of hyper-alert activity every 45–90 minutes for 5, 10, or 15 minutes at a time throughout the day. See if this lowers your stress levels while helping you recover your attention. Additionally, use Power-Pausing to check in to see if you need water, food, a snack, or whatever will help you stay nourished, recharged, and refueled for what's next on your schedule.

PAUSE ON THIS

- How does stress feel in your body?

  _____

  _____

- What's your automatic or default reaction when under pressure?

  _____

  _____

- How would other people describe you when you're stressed?

  _____

  _____

- How would you like to respond to stress to get past the pothole and go in the direction you want to go?

  _____

  _____

CHAPTER 4

The "FUD" Is Real

"We don't just burn out from working too much; we burn out from worrying too much and feeling that we don't matter."

How do you feel given current events or issues happening in your life? Do you wake up feeling *fear*? Are you *uncertain* about the future? Does *doubt* creep into the corners of your life? Or have you gone numb by now?

Most of us experience feelings of fear, uncertainty, and doubt (normally shortened to FUD) in our daily lives and we tend to think we have to suppress, ignore, or reject these powerful feelings. Instead, we can use them as guideposts for better self-care. But first, we need to understand how the FUD is directly affecting us.

FUD surrounds our day-to-day lives and is a factor used by politicians, media, public relations, cults, and social media influencers. It appears in various shapes and sizes as a sales and marketing tactic, negotiation, or even a management ploy to influence, control, and manipulate people. Over the years, the "D" in "FUD" can sometimes stand for "disinformation," which we know intensifies the spread of doubt.

While FUD might be new as part of the self-care conversation, it is a term that has been in our vocabulary since the 1920s and has been used as far back as 1693 as a propaganda tactic. We've become so conditioned to suppressing and ignoring these feelings and we deal with FUD alone or in hiding, but it's costing us sleep, our sense of agency, and our mental health.

In Chapter 3, "Unstress to Get Unstuck," we focused on how stress pushes us to live in survival mode and keeps us stuck. FUD, however, has become that constant stressor in our lives. Between social injustice, a pandemic, mass shootings, and war, day in and day out we are all exposed to circumstances that make us anxious and fearful and with that, uncertain and doubtful about our future. This has allowed us to somewhat drop the facade that everything is okay at work as we realize the need to focus on our shared humanity. The question we are facing now is—do we keep moving toward making work more human? And if so, how do we make sure that we do? We're still behind the learning curve and that's okay. But let's not normalize stress, fear, anxiety, and worry and become numb to these feelings by "just" learning how to manage them. Instead, let's change culture together.

The thing we need to recognize is that we have mental health 24/7. It's not something we have or don't have, something we can turn off and on. The conversation about well-being at work means we need better tools to take care of our mental health, both inside and outside the workplace. The days of separating who we are at work from our personal lives are over, thankfully, because we function best when we're inclusive of who we are as whole human beings—emotions and all. While we might have been aware of FUD in the past and the anxiety we feel, we're just now recognizing its impact on performance and culture, not just on our well-being.

Because of our new hybrid work environment that meshes the personal and professional, we've become more triggered by FUD.

- We *fear* being bypassed if we're not working full time in the office, which challenges our sense of belonging and we question if we are being seen and heard.

- *Uncertainty* about changes in office policies that could affect our ability to work from home (or not) are real because that might affect if we have to change jobs. Additionally, uncertainty around economic circumstances like inflation, recession, and a highly competitive workplace challenges our sense of safety and adds worry about what the future holds.

- *Doubt* about our own performance when we don't have the instant feedback loop that happens in face-to-face environments can trigger our feelings of inadequacy. As a result, our imposter syndrome flares because of the lack of cues to guide us, and we question our ability to achieve our goals.

It's obvious that we need new tools to navigate working remotely, working hybrid, or even working full-time in the office. However, we don't just need "more tech" and new software to be more "efficient" and better manage our time and schedules. We need to access our human advantage by learning the emotional navigation skills that make work and our personal lives more cohesive and enjoyable. The veil may be down, but so are the natural boundaries between our triggers so let's learn how to use them to grow stronger.

FUD and Burnout Go Hand in Hand

FUD tends to make us feel overwhelmed and believe we're broken. Given that our emotions make us human, these aren't feelings to overcome or solve, but advantages to harness and learn from. For instance, it's common belief that we burn out from working too much, but if you pause and think about it, isn't it the worry that really gets to you?

You're not alone. Most people that I've coached through the years assumed they weren't strong or confident enough when they became overwhelmed by FUD. We've even seen an entire movement toward calling people "negative and toxic" and people saying they self-care by letting go of toxic people in their lives. Yes, we need to keep healthy boundaries, but if you ask me, such statements are unhealthy and equally negative and toxic.

What we all need is more care and compassion and better tools to refocus our attention to reclaim agency and get unstuck. We cannot stop the FUD from hitting the fan, but we can stop spinning the fan.

The next time you find your mind stuck in FUD, ask yourself: "What do I need so that I can get past the FUD pothole and feel safe, included, and able?" You might be tempted to think this is moving toward the "power of positive thinking," but that's not the case. Instead it's using the "power of asking better questions" to redirect our attention.

My first burnout came as a result of not respecting my body and its need for water, food, and rest. The second time was when I ran my life on a coffee fix, felt devalued, and consistently worried. In each burnout, my emotions stemming from FUD were the root cause.

What we've failed to realize is that FUD and burnout are close friends and two sides of the same coin. We want to blame it solely on current events or the pandemic, but prior to COVID, 50 percent of the workforce was already on the edge of burnout according to a survey by Deloitte. Once the COVID-19 pandemic hit, it only exacerbated the problem and according to APA (American Psychological Association), the burnout rate jumped to 79 percent, and the World Health Organization (WHO) has established burnout as occupational long-term unmanaged accumulative stress. Companies have increased their well-being program efforts with a focus on mental health to help their people learn how to deal with stress in a more productive and constructive way. I think it's important that we don't expect our work and life to be stress-free but rather learn that we don't have to be stressed out by stressful events. Being more inclusive of our emotional and mental health at work, we can prevent burnout by having the tools and skills to face our emotions in a healthy manner.

That's why a vacation won't solve our FUD problems.

When I speak with leaders about this, they pause and reflect on the fact that work-life balance isn't the solution to the issue at hand. Their eyes have to be opened to the idea that changing the way we think and engage with each other is key to cultivating a healthy work culture. To be clear, I'm not suggesting that we don't need more time off. We do. But it only works if we can suspend our worries during our time away and not end up returning to work feeling overwhelmed, fearful, and uncertain, and then have to navigate disrespectful interpersonal relationships within the first few hours.

It's rare to find someone who hasn't felt exhausted at some point over the last few years. A big reason many feel this way is because of the added workload of homeschooling and chores—especially for women—throughout the pandemic, and the pressure hasn't let up. It forced many to leave the workforce because it was not humanly possible to do it all. While the pandemic is partly to blame, many companies have long before this cultivated a competitive burnout culture built on FUD in pursuit of peak performance. It's more evident than ever that the way we work needs an upgrade. This is one of several reasons a healthy work culture and work-life quality are vital to our personal health and well-being. They affect our work and interpersonal relationships, making it a two-way street.

When the Great Resignation kicked off in 2021, it consisted of people either leaving a toxic work culture or resigning themselves to stay in one for as long as they could hold on. The question we *need* to ask, however, is whether we're working in a toxic hustle culture driven by FUD to get people to work harder, or if we're working in a care-driven culture where FUD is recognized as an opportunity to discuss what we each need to work more effectively?

The key to dealing with FUD is learning how to deal with it and cultivate a culture where it becomes something we face together rather than ignore. The problem we're facing at work is that we've become conditioned to hide from FUD, pretending that it doesn't affect us. By doing so, our actions leave us burnt out, cost us our health, paralyze our productivity, and hamstrings our culture.

To move forward, let's engage our curiosity and face the FUD.

Moving from FUD to Agency Takes Curiosity

Growing up, the stoic image of my great grandfather and grandfather taught me that FUD was to be ignored, whereas, for my mother, it overwhelmed her life. My father, however, taught me to navigate the FUD by facing it.

My mom struggled with depression and bipolar disorder, so FUD was a genuine struggle inside our household. While my mom managed great externally, when something changed in her environment she didn't feel she could control, she'd fall apart internally. On a personal level, after surviving a car crash with my dad when I was seven years old, my face being stitched back together without anesthesia, and not being allowed to have my dad present during the process, I became overwhelmed by the fear of being alone. This was intensified by my mother's fear of losing me, as this was already my third brush with death in my short time on the planet.

When FUD would hit me as a child, my dad would sit with me and ask me to tell him all about it. He'd then ask what the worst thing that could happen might be. After imagining and communicating my worst-case scenario, he would listen and acknowledge my fears before asking me what I'd do if they became a reality. To this day, I still remember coming up with all the ways I could solve the problems. Then I'd look to him, wondering if my solutions would work. My dad would just smile and assure me that now I knew what to do if the worst occurred. Then he'd conclude by reminding me it probably wouldn't happen and encourage me to grow courageous and chase after what I wanted to do.

The relief my father's guidance gave me was immediate because our conversations, and the skills he taught me, gave me a sense of agency and control. By simply asking questions, he sparked my curiosity, which allowed clarity and courage to develop, including a path forward. Years later, I discovered that what I learned is neurobiology, mindfulness, hypnotherapy, and self-coaching all in one.

When we are stuck in fear, uncertainty, and doubt about the future, our curiosity, clarity, and courage get crushed. When we ask questions that direct our attention past the FUD toward where we want to go, we develop a sense of agency and hope.

FUD Is an Opportunity for Change

Human beings are *full* of questions. It's how we navigate life. Our mind constantly thinks and processes whether we're aware of it or not. According to some research, we make upward of 35,000 decisions a day, with 95 percent of them being an unconscious automatic reaction.

When asking questions, the brain automatically looks for an answer, which basically hijacks our attention. Many of us believe we can multi-task multiple questions, but we can't. We can only think about one idea at a time. So when FUD takes us over, then that's all we notice. If you've ever wondered how anxiety can turn into a full-blown panic attack, this is how.

Your mind will always try to answer the question you ask and it will look anywhere and everywhere to find the answer. A question that you cannot answer because it's about the future and therefore unknown makes you basically feel that you have no agency or control. This is probably why so many would like to have a psychic on hand when we need to know what this hypothetical future will be like. Questions like that lead us to feeling a loss of control rather than actually finding a "constructive" answer.

Our mind is extremely powerful and believes what we tell it, and this is how we can utilize visualization to become comfortable with a hypothetical future and create change. In 2018, I spoke at an event in Brazil about mindfulness and health where Ellen Langer, a professor of psychology at Harvard University, also spoke. She shared the results of her Counterclockwise study, which she conducted in 1979, about the power of the mind. Her study consisted of a group of elderly men who were tasked with living for one week as if it were 1959. She created an environment that brought them back to how they lived 20 years earlier. The music they listened to, the decor, the TV shows, their clothing, and even the food they ate matched this previous time period. At the end of the study, after just one week, she could see how their aging had reversed and their overall health and mental agility had improved.

The power of our mind is incredible, and we can learn how to use it to work better for us, solve the problems and navigate the FUD that we will continue to face in our daily lives. The key is not to unlock the stress cycle so it doesn't take us into a tail-spin but rather we learn how to stand in the storm without being blown over. There's a Buddhist saying: "Peace comes from within, do not seek it without."

Intention Fuels Attention

The way we ask questions directs our attention. When we change the question, we change the outcome because our mind will look for the answer we tell it to look for. For example, if you ask why something is *not* working, you'll discover answers that confirm why something isn't working. In the same way when we ask, "What's wrong with me?" we end up finding the answers that confirm our fears which can make us feel even more "wrong.

Source: Path For Life®

To see this in action, imagine if I said to you, "Do *not* think about a polar bear waving at you." What are you thinking about now? I show an image of this example in my keynotes, and everyone in the audience confirms that they cannot shake the image of the waving polar bear. Essentially, the way we ask questions and speak to ourselves all day long is self-hypnosis. In hypnotherapy, we avoid using "not" because we don't register the word and only register the action words that come after it. Simply put, when I say: "Do not think about a polar bear waving at you," what your subconscious mind hears is "think about a polar bear waving at you."

If instead I said, "Imagine a polar bear in striped trunks on the beach playing with a beach ball," I'm willing to bet that you have already visualized that image, even though it's not real. You might have even started thinking about what color the beach ball is. At least you have now. That's the power of suggestion. And it's also the power of questions. The way we ask questions fuels our attention and this is how we can refocus our mind toward accessing our own inner resources, get unstuck, and move forward.

Our Three Basic Questions

We have three different parts of the brain that we use interchangeably, without even knowing it. The conscious mind, the subconscious mind, and the unconscious mind. To start taking advantage of our human ability to use our mind productively and constructively, Power-Pausing is the essential tool that helps us access our so-called "higher-executive function," also called the "smart brain," where we make better decisions.

But first, let's get to know the different areas of the brain and how the way we ask questions can help us direct our attention. Each part of the brain is connected to either survival mode, connection mode, and/or constructive-solution mode. As a result, when navigating through life, we focus on three main questions: "Am I safe?" "Do I belong?" and "What can I learn from this?"

"Am I Safe?"

The unconscious mind is the reactive mind, also called the "brainstem." This is the part of our mind that's running our automatic unconscious behaviors that make up about 95 percent of our mindset. It's connected to our survival instincts, and therefore, triggered by FUD. When we are under stress and cortisol is high, this part of the brain is automatically focused on the question: "Am I safe?"

Perhaps you can imagine how exhausted you would be if you were to consciously ask yourself if you were safe all day long. Your attention would essentially be focused on everything that's wrong and dangerous around you. On one hand, this has helped us survive evolution. But on the other hand, it can also evoke survival stress, which is when cortisol flares and takes over our mind. If cortisol stays chronically high, we can end up stuck in this survival-mode mindset, which can not only be debilitating, but can also lead to burnout.

What also happens at this stage is we react to triggers and our focus narrows on just getting through the day, which means we lose out on connection and creativity. We end up pushing harder to control a situation that's not working, ignore cues, and basically hope we make it through the storm. While there has been extensive research on this topic, it's not important to dwell on the data here. The key to reclaiming agency over this stress mode is to pause so that we can recognize *when* it happens and then we can use the power of asking better questions to get unstuck.

Once we pause and recognize that we're in a FUD spiral, we can take a few deep breaths to calm down our nervous system, slow our thoughts, and reset our intention, which then refuels our attention to a more productive mindset. It might be as simple as grabbing some water to come out of survival-mode and pausing ourselves from the feeling that we're running for our lives.

"Do I Belong?"

Once we can come out of survival mode, our intention shifts to being emotionally and socially safe and our need to connect with others is the intention that fuels our attention. We are more present and start engaging our subconscious mind, also called the "emotional brain," where the question that directs our attention is, "Do I belong?"

Our need to belong makes us look for cues that we are seen, heard, included, and that we matter. This is an unchanging part of human nature that is part of our survival-mode response as feeling emotionally safe is crucial to our physical health. The more we communicate, observe, and engage to ensure we are included and belong, the more we feel like we're part of a community.

Because we look for cues and feedback from others, we naturally wonder if people like us and whether we are being listened to. It's the emotional part of the brain that's active but also often the subconscious mind, which is why we need to learn to Power-Pausing so that we can better engage in a more mindful and constructive way. We want to participate and contribute so we can more actively pay attention to each other and observe our relationships to make them more consciously meaningful. This is just one of many reasons why self-care isn't just about us, but about our connection with others, too.

"What Can I Learn from This?"

When we use Power-Pausing to come out of survival mode and we feel emotionally and socially safe, we can start to access the third level of the brain called the prefrontal cortex, which is our problem-solving mind, the cognitive, regulating, and executive functioning state of the brain. We can now use the way we ask questions to be curious and constructive and we consciously direct our questions and ask, "What can I learn from this?"

This is where we tap into our ability to adapt and harness change so that we can grow. We become creative and constructive, and we ask questions that keep us exploring possibilities and guide us toward effective problem solving and innovation.

I'm not talking about results here. I mean learning. Growth is emotional, spiritual, and mental. It's about growing relationships, our skills, and an ability to keep building a life we love, which is inclusive of all our three core relationships—the one we have with ourselves, others, and work. Because whether or not we want to admit it, they go hand-in-hand to develop who we are.

USE YOUR MIND TO WORK BETTER FOR YOU
PREVENTING BURNOUT & HARNESSING OUR HUMAN ADVANTAGE TO CARE

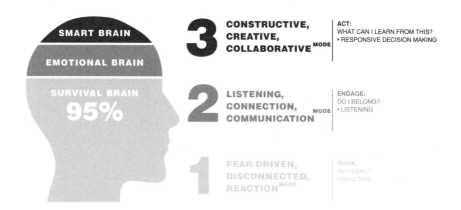

Source: Path For Life®

Working with the Fear

One of my fears is people climbing ladders. When I was a kid getting ready for school one morning, I heard my dad yelling for help in the house we were building. The ladder we'd been using to get upstairs and downstairs while waiting for our staircase to be completed had gone out from under him. My dad, in a suit and holding his briefcase in one hand, held on for dear life with his other hand to avoid falling.

I also have a fear of falling down the stairs. I fell down a set of stairs from running too fast as a child, and it's also happened as an adult when I tripped. Because I live alone, I still find myself being nervous of falling with no one to help me. It happened to my grandmother, who had to wait until my grandfather got home and could take her to the hospital.

You probably have rational and irrational fears too. Despite these fears being part of daily life, we cannot live in fear, but rather learn from them and use them to hone our mindfulness. For instance, because of my fear of falling downstairs, I ask myself, "What do I need to feel safe so that I can get hold of someone?" Thankfully, we now have voice-controlled devices that allow us to call for help when needed. I also take simple precautions like paying attention and holding handrails. I never wear socks that make the stairs more slippery, and I slow down when on stairs. Instead of living in fear, I live with basic awareness.

Learning to reclaim agency over my own emotional and mental health when circumstances are not within my control is a deep training of trust that's become essential for my life. It has helped me be mindful about how I navigate change in order to grow with curiosity and courage. The more we see our fears and accept the FUD as part of society and the cultural landscape, the better we are able to be aware, adaptable, and agile in navigating it.

The reality is we can rarely control our circumstances, but we can choose how we respond. Choosing how we respond to crises is a key factor in reclaiming agency, as it helps us to focus on what is happening, rather than getting stuck in what we wish would happen. We have cute acronyms for fear like—"false evidence appearing real"—that can appear to be more about "manhandling" our emotions as opposed to letting them inform us. We can't ignore our fears, nor succumb to them despite ongoing challenges in the modern world. Instead, the hardships give us an opportunity we cannot shirk, which is why we must rethink self-care. It's not just about preventing burnout, keeping employees engaged, and ensuring we're healthy and motivated. It's about fostering work-life quality because work will never be the same, and we can no longer ignore that FUD is part of our lives.

What we need is to cultivate the space to discuss how we can be inclusive of our emotional and mental health at work while also asking questions that help us gain new skills and tools to face the FUD. We need this for ourselves, our communities, and our companies.

It's important we pause together in order to rethink what matters and what we care about. In the past, we might have ignored or pushed our feelings aside as we do with our self-care while rushing to get work done. Now we have the opportunity to be inclusive, create change, and grow together. That's why I think of self-care as a conversation we not only have with ourselves but also the conversations we have with each other and therefore how we collaborate and make better decisions together.

In the second part of this book, we'll learn how to use questions to get unstuck and cut through the overwhelming feelings of FUD so that we can navigate change and harness growth.

To me, that's the most self-caring we can be—*to ask better questions.*

PAUSE ON THIS

- What are your typical FUD triggers? For example, one of mine is reading the news.

  _____

  _____

- In what ways do you normally deal with your FUD feelings?

  _____

  _____

(continued)

(continued)

- What are some FUD patterns you recognize when communicating with other people?

  _____

  _____

- How would you like to face the FUD in your life?

  _____

  _____

CHAPTER 5

Rethinking Time

"Self-care doesn't take time away from us; it gives us time back because it's how we spend time better."

A broadcasting executive came to me on the edge of burnout saying she felt physically, emotionally, and mentally drained. Getting out of bed in the morning had become a challenge while at the same time, she had trouble sleeping through the night. She was constantly anxious and scared, feeling like everything could fall apart at any moment. On top of this, she knew she had been consistently short and impatient with her team and her partner. She was a classic example of someone operating out of a place of chronic survival mode; her body was failing her, and she knew she couldn't keep up this pace much longer.

I agreed with her, given that she did absolutely nothing to self-care throughout the day—not even the basics. She didn't pause for water or food or even take a moment to breathe. Instead, she lived on coffee as she moved from task to task. Her mind was constantly spinning, stuck in all the problems, focused on what wasn't working.

I asked her to make sure she drank water throughout the day as dehydration alone can cause anxiety, a sense of being over-whelmed, brain fog, fatigue, and irritability. Taking consistent water breaks is the most essential and simplest self-care tool and performance hack we have. I also asked her to respect her lunch break and eat some real food instead of resorting to eating a protein-bar on the run. She resisted saying she didn't have time. I reminded her that she didn't have time *not* to as it was clear to both her and me that she was breaking down. Instead of forcing herself to work harder, I asked her to pause and recognize that she needed her body to work for her, as much as her body needed her to take care of it.

She finally admitted that since her boss wasn't taking lunch, she didn't feel she could either. I empathized with that because during my time as a fashion executive, I too had to fight for my right to have lunch. So, I asked her to stand up for herself and tell her manager that she needed to take the time to eat.

I'm sharing this story because this woman is not alone. Not by a long shot. So many of us skip breakfast because we sleep as late as humanly possible. Then we grab coffee to get rid of the brain fog as we run out the door and eat protein bars or snacks on the go and call it lunch before downing more coffee to numb the hunger. By evening, we crash after scarfing down dinner and maybe a drink or two to calm down, only to fall asleep and wake up a few hours later with our mind racing, wondering what we might have missed and worried about what we have to get done.

For my client though, only two weeks after leaning into the basics of water, food, and breaks throughout the day, which all also helped her get a good night's sleep, she told me she felt so much better.

- She had more energy, she felt more focused, she could hold her attention for much longer, and she was not as easily distracted.

- Her mood was better and she was more patient while being less irritable.

- She felt less anxious and more productive. She even felt more confident, courageous, and clear-headed when making decisions.

- She felt less overwhelmed even though her workload had not changed, and she didn't crash as hard at night when coming home resulting in an improved relationship with her partner.

Just water, lunch, and getting a good nights' sleep. Not some fancy new self-care routine, just simple essential sustenance that kept her whole body system from running on survival mode. Today, my client thinks of her daily energy management as regenerative rather than depleting. Not only that, but since she started to take lunch, so did the rest of her team. As a result, team-work improved and so did their collective performance.

We are trying to keep up with the speed of technology by working harder, but we cannot hack time by abandoning our self-care. Even though we work with computers, we have to remind ourselves that we are not like them, and we are not supposed to be. Tech is there to support us in working better and our job is to support our whole human system all day long in working better too. Self-care is actually an investment in our work as it allows us to hit the sweet spot where we have clarity, energy, vibrancy, strength, resilience, empathy, patience, and an overall better mood.

Source: Path For Life®

Many people say they don't have time for self-care; I say they don't have time not to. My client that I just mentioned is just one of many who realized that when you make self-care proactive and the foundation of your day, it creates *more* time—because it's how we spend time better and it's how we achieve our goals without burning out.

"Yes, but I Don't Have Time"

For the last 18 years, I've been coaching people and speaking at companies about how we can rethink self-care at work to reclaim agency and cultivate a better work-life quality. Though the faces and circumstances change, one thing that hasn't is that no matter where I am and who I'm speaking to, from CEOs to recent grads, I still hear "Yes, but..." all the time. "Yes, but I don't have time...," "Yes, but I need to get this done, then I can...," "Yes, but you don't understand, I have to...."

Without even realizing it, whenever work gets stressful, we put ourselves, our relationships, our health, and our work-life quality on hold—which isn't at all our fault but rather our social construct.

I have consistently seen that we want to take better care of ourselves, but work gets in the way, and we default to putting it first, our friends and family next, and ourselves last. When working with clients who'd been diagnosed with life-threatening illnesses, they still struggled with guilt to prioritize their health and well-being even though their life literally depended on it. It's a complete misunderstanding of what work needs from us and what we need from work. It's why, in this book, we are rethinking the impact of self-care on our three core relationships of self, others, and work.

We all know we cut corners when we are tired. We all also know we become irritable and short with people when we are hangry, and we dismiss our family or snap at the kids a bit too fast when we are under stress. It's okay to admit we act like this because we are all human. Admitting this is the first step to change and a big part of this is how we view our relationship with time.

It's a Matter of Time

A client told me that he wished he could stop working and was looking for an exit strategy. I asked him to pause and consider what kind of exit strategy he was looking for, to which he replied, "I want to retire. But I'm one of three partners at the firm, and it will just not work without me. I feel stuck and like I need to keep going."

The man had built the company with his partners and all of them had become society's view of successful. But at the same time, the days were stressful and this lifestyle of putting work above all else had taken a toll on both his mental well-being and physical health.

At the time of speaking to him, he was more than 150 pounds overweight and both his blood pressure and cholesterol were through the roof. Like a lot of people, he lived on coffee, and at the end of his non-stop days, he downed a big meal and chased it with a few too many scotches. On top of this, even when he was with his family, he was glued to his phone responding to emails and texts. For my client, it was no longer about making more money. He wanted time off and he wanted a better work-life quality.

I asked him if the exit strategy he was looking for might be the heart attack his doctor had warned him about, which got his attention.

"You might be right," he said after taking a pause and looking at me for several minutes with concerned eyes. "I'm looking for an excuse to stop working, but it's up to me to change the way I work because work is not going to slow down for me."

Sometimes it's only a matter of time before life will force us to care about ourselves, so let's stop "Yes, but-ing" ourselves, and instead, reclaim time with self-care.

Work Needs to Be Inclusive of What We Care About

I learned the hard way that "Yes, but-ing" doesn't work. My mom and dad split time between living in Denmark and living with me in New York City, while at the same time, they were both going through cancer therapy in two different countries. During this period in my life, work demanded everything from me and in return, I gave all my attention back to it. My mom asked me several times if we could go Christmas shopping or have lunch together as we usually did but that particular year, I just didn't have the time. Between their treatment schedules, the work on my plate, and my team constantly nagging me when I wasn't working, I "Yes but-ed," my mom several times until she stopped asking. Like a lot of moms, she said she understood, but I knew it made her sad, and yet I still chose to focus on work. It turned out to be our last Christmas together.

Had I known, I would have made different choices. But that's the problem, isn't it? We do not always know, and we prioritize our duty to work first, only to wake up one day and realize it's too late.

That's a survival-mode mindset running our lives.

When my mom died suddenly while I was at work, I wrapped up my upcoming tasks, briefed my team, and went home to prepare to tell my dad as he was set to arrive later that evening from Denmark to continue his own treatment. In the end, my mom died alone while I was at work and my dad was on a plane. I had no clue she was that ill because I was too preoccupied with work.

After I returned to the office two weeks after her passing, I was fired. The leadership team figured that since I now had to be the caregiver for my dad on my own, I wouldn't have enough time for work. Of course, this wasn't the official reason, but one of the owners let it slip one day by mistake. Having my eyes opened to the fact I wasn't as needed and indispensable as I thought turned out to be a big lesson in setting boundaries. It made me realize that work has to work for me too and not just me working for the company.

This experience hurt. But I'm glad it happened. I was no longer going to "Yes, but" my health, life, and those I care about; it had to be an all-inclusive package.

Rethinking Boundaries: Changing What "On Company Time" Means

The lines between work and life have become blurred; we work all the time, even when we are not "at work" because tech means we are always available. During COVID, many of us were living at work 24/7, and work habits were beginning to get out of control. While we thought we just had to push through for the short term, it became apparent after the first year that we had to keep going, indefinitely. That's when we started saying, "We just need to be more resilient." But because we think of resilience as biting down, shutting up and keeping going, it has worn us out. Now, we can finally start asking questions about what we need to change in the way we work so we can navigate the reality we are in, instead of just waiting for things to "go back to normal" because let's face it—that didn't work either.

Some countries, companies, and states in the United States are looking at implementing a four-day work week as studies have shown that we not only get the same amount of work done, but we are also even more productive. Many companies have created no-meeting Fridays to give their people a chance to catch up and avoid "Zoom fatigue" because so many of us have ended up living on endless virtual meetings.

We have to pause and ask ourselves: "Is this our new work style?" And if so, how do we make it sustainable?

When I work with companies to create a healthier work culture, I see the initiative to change the corporate meeting calendar to include pauses between meetings, which is a great recognition that we need micro-pauses to manage stress. But this will only work if we choose to spend that time prepping our whole human system for the next meeting instead of spending it answering emails. We do this by pausing to reconnect with what we each need to keep ourselves supported throughout the day. It's not just a moment in time to get our documents in order or reply to messages. It's a moment in time to get ready to pay attention again, so we bring our full presence to the next meeting.

As much as we are seeing more flexibility around when and where we work, it's still up to us to turn off, breathe, and reset.

In her book, *Peak Mind,* neuroscientist, Amishi P. Jha, PhD, shares that studies have shown that 50 percent of the time our mind wanders off and doesn't stay engaged with what is going on right in front of us. As she says, "We are missing half of our lives." Can you imagine the amazing possibility this is for activating a care-driven mindset? This is exactly why it's so vital that we learn to use Power-Pausing to be inclusive of our human needs rather than continuing to ignore ourselves. We think that we are saving time, but we're not. We need a self-care mindset instead to master our energy, attention, and focus.

No matter how quickly technological advancements are coming at us, work isn't about keeping up with the speed of technology—as that's a race we can't possibly win. Today, we are in a care-driven economy—a relationship economy—where it's the quality of our human relationships at work that matters most, which includes not only the ones we have with our clients and with each other, but also the relationship we have with ourselves.

Rethinking how we spend our time working is crucial to work-life quality because it's not how fast and hard we work that makes us great, it's who we are that makes us great.

PAUSE ON THIS

- When do you reach a point where you become resentful that you have too much on your plate?

  _____

  _____

- What kind of situations trigger you to let your boundaries slip?

  _____

  _____

- What kind of situations make it easier for you to keep healthy boundaries?

  _____

  _____

CHAPTER 6

Rethinking Peak Performance

"Peak performance isn't about doing more, working harder and faster; it's about working better by pausing to make better decisions that are aligned with what we care about."

Do you feel beat up and worn out by the end of the day? You are not alone. We are living in a culture where performance is seen as going hard at it, full on, undivided attention, 100 percent commitment, and nothing else matters. Some people dread the pressure; others thrive on the adrenalin rush. It's like the boxer going into the ring to fight, except we do it every day. We get into the ring, put our heads down, and fight. We just have to stand till the end of the day, we just have to go another round, and another round and another round, then we will win. It's the image of resilience and performance that we replayed in our heads during the pandemic too, isn't it? We just have to keep going, keep standing, to get through.

Except there's something we tend to forget when we watch a boxing match. We focus so much on the fight, how fast the steps are and how strong the punches are, that we forget what really gets the boxer through the fight. The boxers go to the corner for a one-minute Power-Pausing every three minutes, to reset, recover, refocus, and reclaim their intention, attention, focus, and energy. Without the Power-Pausing, the fighters would not get through the fight, at least not at their best.

So can we all agree we need to rethink performance? Reality is that even if we are paid for the results we create, they are achieved by being more mindful about the work we do and conscious about the decisions we make. The question to ask isn't how we can work faster; the question is how can we work better? What do we need so that we can tap into our human advantage?

When I was six years old, I was chosen for the competitive gymnastics team in Denmark. Even at such a young age, it was downright intense. Training sessions involved 15 minutes of running to warm up, 30 minutes of stretching and calisthenics to strengthen our bodies, then practicing gymnastic jumps and movements that we would carry out during the competition, before finishing with a solid stretching session to wind down.

On top of this, we performed the entire two-and-a-half hour session without much talking. Our trainer wanted us to avoid getting distracted by chatter. If we took a week off, we were told it would take us two weeks to get back into shape. It was like a boot camp for kids.

Why am I telling you the details of how we spent the time? Because peak performance is rooted in the preparation and the practice. In our training, we spent just as much time getting our bodies and minds ready as we did in practicing the jumps. Being in competition-type shape meant the continued process of getting stronger and more flexible while developing a focused mindset.

Looking back, it was a good way to grow up. Winning was something we did together and the same goes for the feelings of shame we experienced when one of us would misstep a jump as our individual actions affected the entire team's score. Like a lot of competitive people, I would strive to be the best on the team but I never reached the number one position, and as a team, we usually came in second as well. I used my size as an excuse for not being the best as I was taller than the other girls. However, there's a bit of a reckoning that has taken place as I've matured. First, despite my coach's effort to have me focus on the process to get my sought-after results, I focused too much on the result of winning. Second, I also realized I craved winning for the wrong reasons as I interpreted it as a way to be admired and liked as that was my version of belonging.

In my career in the fashion business, I could see the same mindset driving me at work. Later with my coaching clients, I consistently saw the same desire to win as the drive that fueled performance, growth, and success in them.

Speaking with leaders every day who are teetering on the edge of burnout, it's obvious that we need to recognize the relationship between preparation, process, and presence to reach peak performance in the workplace. We focus on achieving our goals at work but tend to forget to include what we need as human beings in order to achieve our goals. Though the situation is not the same, just like how athletes use their bodies and minds to keep improving their performance, we do as well. It's time we recognize the importance of treating the health of our bodies and mind as the foundation for daily peak performance in the workplace.

Working Harder or Working Better?

We see companies issue rewards to the highest achievers, the best score, or those who bring in the highest amount of revenue. It's a hustle environment, which often becomes a toxic competition against each other as opposed to a team-focused effort on growth. We hear stories of peak performers who can handle more and get a lot done, and it's easy to think that's what we have to do as well. After all, performance has long been stuck in the principle of doing more and achieving more.

This focus on results over process tends to mean long hours, a race against time, and the abandonment of self-care to save time. We see this in start-ups, entrepreneurs, and young people who are starting their careers with the ambition to excel and climb the corporate ladder. It also shows up during times of product launches, crises, transitions, and mergers. It's a hustle culture where people burn out instead of growing and thriving because the underlying mindset is that we need to just keep going until we achieve our results and reach success—no matter what we do to get there.

You probably know the inner dialog that comes along with focusing on results—"I'm not doing enough!" "I'm not working enough!" "I'll miss something important if I ease up!" It can quickly become a constant state of being overwhelmed in an effort to reach your goals. The problem is this approach is a never-ending race for more instead of better—which is the exact opposite of top athletes who focus on the process of getting better instead of doing more. They use rest and recovery to support the effectiveness of putting in the reps.

This mindset of *more, more, more,* and *never being, doing, or having enough* is costing us our mental health. We see this every-where. Even athletes are speaking up about what happens when they lose their joy due to the demands and pressures put on them. We need to get back to the point where joy is found in striving for our peak performance and not just in striving to reach the results others expect of us, hoping that joy will follow.

This may make me sound like I don't like peak performance. But this isn't the case; I love it. What's needed, though, is a rethink to understand what truly drives us to perform at our best and what peak performance really means in today's work environment.

Peak performance driven by self-care means to build on our strengths by asking what we need to achieve our goals. Rather than abandoning our most basic human needs of water, food, and sleep, we use our bodies and minds to get us there. It's important to make it clear that self-care is not the goal here—but rather, it's how we support ourselves in reaching our goals. And this starts with understanding ourselves and consistently asking what we need to perform better.

Instead of continuing to push ourselves to achieve, Power-Pausing is how we stop for a moment to listen inside and get clear on what we need to climb the mountain in front of us with the proper training, skills, and equipment.

My dad was an avid runner, and I would often run with him. He always ran barefoot in the sand and he talked about being relaxed to be able to run long distances. He used to sprint when he was younger and then ran marathons later on. He always told me to relax my muscles to let the blood flow while running and how to have an inner dialog that was like a mantra to keep my focus. Recently, I heard about how legendary coach Bud Winter trained his runners in this way, teaching them self-hypnosis and to focus on loose hands, a relaxed jaw, and an open chest. I'm sure my dad had read Winter's book, *Relax and Win*, since my dad's attitude to running was the same. The interesting thing about this is that it supports the mind and body's natural ability to perform better and for longer when we are not clenched down in fear, but rather enjoying the process. I always used to wonder why so many people would smile at me while I was running in the street, and one day I realized it was probably because I was smiling. When we clench down to push on we increase inflammation in the body. But when we open up our heart and mind, breathe and let the blood flow, we access the real power we hold inside, our inner fuel.

The challenge we see at work is that we tighten up, and instead of pausing to listen and ask what we need so that we can get through when we get busy or stressed, we abandon ourselves and resort to our old training and automatic habits, driven by survival mode. To stop burning out and to start working better, we cannot keep doing what we've always done. Instead, to create positive change, we must first change the way we think, which means recognizing that self-care is a skill too.

When it comes to implementing self-care, we need to realize that performing at our best is not about constantly pushing hard or doing more but rather the foundation for being able to think better, engage better, and make better and faster decisions. When we can cut through the noise of our inner dialog, ask better questions, and get to the crux of the matter, we can be more constructive and creative in the way we solve problems while helping us align with the core objective and purpose that we are working toward—aka, the result we want to achieve.

Think about situations when you have been stressed, exhausted, hangry, dehydrated, and ended up making a rash decision only to realize that you had not paused to think it through properly. Think about moments when you pushed yourself harder than normal to achieve a result without pausing to consider if that was really the result you needed to achieve to make something work in the first place. Lastly, consider when you have been so focused on getting your desired result that you missed cues along the way that could have been used to produce a better result.

Just while writing this book, a chief financial officer shared with me how he'd fallen in love with Wordle. During this love affair, something interesting popped out. He realized on the days he got stuck on a word and walked away frustrated, the next time he came back to it, the answer was obvious. It was the stepping away that changed the focus and attention that created results. When people tell me they don't have time to pause, I tell them they don't have time not to.

Performance Is About Being Happy

We expect a lot of ourselves. Social norms and the constant exposure to the success of others on social media are taking a toll on our mental health because the underlying message is to do more and then do more again to measure up. With the expectation to always do more and be perfect at it, no matter the circumstance, we tend to give work our all instead of our best. But will we ever be or feel like we're enough if we continue to view growth as more? Probably not. Unfortunately though, it's weaved into the web of school, work, and life. Even our vacations have become about more. However, this mindset of seeing abundance as "more" instead of better is a battle that we will never win, nor is it a healthy one. As a society, partially thanks to COVID, we are starting to question this constant pursuit of more, especially as consumption is straining our global health and social injustice and inequity have become part of our daily concerns.

Companies are thankfully starting to recognize that performance and productivity can no longer be measured by results alone but rather by understanding how we work better as whole humans. We see how the interview process is focused around personality traits rather than just the results we have achieved in the past. It's the shift to understanding the importance of *how* we reach our results that matters: how we think, how we engage with each other, and how we make decisions. Managers are learning that if they only ask why something is not done yet, instead of asking what someone needs so they can get it done, they are not helping their people achieve results.

When we are unhappy, we don't perform well. When we don't feel appreciated and valued, we don't perform well. And when we don't have direction and know the expectations of what good looks like, we don't perform well. To make this change, it's important that we pause and acknowledge that now is the moment in time to rethink work and ask what success looks like and what we need to perform at our best.

According to the latest research from the University of Warwick, happiness makes people more productive at work. Economists carried out a number of studies to learn if happy employees work better and they found that happiness made people around 12 percent more productive.

Purpose, Goals, and Rethinking What Matters

As we are entering a post-COVID work culture—at least one where we know how to handle the potential oncoming new variants—many of us are asking questions like, "How do I want to live my life now?" "What is enough?" and "What makes me happy?"

And that's a good thing.

I ask myself these questions on a regular basis as a way to observe, evaluate, and decide what a good life feels and looks like to me.

The way I reach my goals makes a difference between a work-life that costs me my health and one that grows my joy and maintains my health. I always consider my ambitions for my work as part of my daily life, not separate from it. I also ask myself questions like:

- "What do I enjoy doing?"

- "What are my strengths?"

- "What drains me and why? Is it because I'm scared because it's new and unfamiliar?"

- "How do I want to spend my days?"

- "How do I do my best work?" "Is it on my own or as part of a team?"

- "In what kind of work environment do I function best, and when do I function best?"

- "What do I need in my day to support myself in doing my best work?"

What you might have noticed is I ask questions from a place of curiosity to learn more about myself. The key to progress is asking constructive questions—ones that help you discover the path forward and connects with what you care about. It is what makes you tick that's the clue to happiness and learning what you need is how you can pursue a life where work doesn't hurt but instead fuels you.

Peak Performance Comes from What We Care About

What do you care about?

When I ask people what they care about, they often say they don't know. And I don't know about you, but this is scary. We've resigned ourselves to the way things are and become numb to recognizing what drives us because it has become normal to work in survival mode and to be driven by what frightens us. We want to know how to care again.

Fear is, and has always been, part of the human drive. However, it's not what makes us perform at our best. Many "old-style" leaders still drive a hard-core, result-driven, hustle approach to peak performance and they think that being people-driven means more benefits and higher rewards. But they are so wrong. It hurts me to think about how they must struggle to keep their people engaged, committed, and motivated to produce results when they don't know what drives their people. Working in push-push-push mode is excellent when facing a deadline—and we all have to work in sprints at times for a couple of days. But problems arise when our primary driver is pushing ourselves to meet the deadline as opposed to being driven by making things happen that matter. The former wears us down and leads to burn-out; the latter fuels us.

So, what do you care about?

I'm asking again because I want you to pause for a moment and look at the pattern of what drives you. Is it fear or desire? Do you wake up in the morning and immediately feel anxious about the day ahead and already feel scared that you won't get what you need to get done? Or do you get up curious about what each day will bring?

I know, the latter is a BIG ask these days. And it's one of the reasons we're seeing the Great Resignation unfold. We have either resigned ourselves to exist to do a job that is running us down or we are leaving our jobs in pursuit of work we care about that aligns with our values at companies that care about us too.

Peak Performance Equity

Before we go any further though, I want to talk about privilege here. We cannot all do the work we love. Not all of us have the resources, background, family, or societal support to achieve the privilege to do work that we love.

Many people have not been able to receive the education that would afford them the opportunity to pursue work they truly care about. Some have had to start working right out of school to support their loved ones if they were fortunate to get an education at all. There are many reasons why someone has not enjoyed the possibilities that others have, and I ask that there is no judgment about the choices someone has made or has had to make to survive.

Race, gender, gender identities, neuro-diversities, and disabilities are all aspects of our shared human reality that play into finding a way to discuss peak performance from a place of accessibility, respect, and equity.

There is no question that we need to shift from a hustle culture to a human-driven culture; the question is how, not as a general question, but as an individualized one. I hope that we can start thinking in a more equitable way when we discuss how to support people at work so that we understand their individual challenges and support them where they are by giving them tools to reclaim agency over their lives. We can't assume that peak performance looks the same for everyone because it doesn't.

Depression is another aspect of not being able to tap into what we care about, and we will continue to discuss mental health in this book. However, we are not going to address mental illness. It would not be fair to those who struggle every day to believe that a book about self-care at work can solve that. That said, I hope the conversation about cultivating mental health can be helpful. Growing up with a mom who struggled with bipolar disorder, I believe many of the tools in this book can help since I have developed them with her in mind.

The last point I will make here is that the pandemic has challenged us as people and workers differently. Single parents have taken on what has felt like extra jobs. We know that nearly 3 million American women have left the workforce because they were hit harder by furloughs, lay-offs, and the sheer magnitude of tackling work and childcare during the pandemic. Additionally, families who take care of aging parents have seen the added layer of stress, especially women caregivers, even if they've had their partners help and support. Lastly, frontline healthcare workers and other essential services have carried a burden of both their fears and ours.

But what does look the same to each of us is our human need to access peak performance in a way that's not fear-driven and leads to burn out, but one that is care-driven and leads to joy.

We Each Value and Care About Different Things

Peak performance means different things to different people. In this new world, we must understand the need to be inclusive of our self-care, who we are, what we care about, what our boundaries are, and what support system we can put in place. Just pushing harder to achieve is not sustainable, and it's also not what work is about anymore. We want our workplace to respect and care about who we are, and we want our work to fulfill us and grow our sense of self as it aligns with what matters to us.

The new questions we are asking are not just about growth opportunities, benefits, and rewards. But rather, we want to know if the company we work at has our back, if they value work-life balance, if they actively support work-life quality, and actually support a healthy culture and it's not just used as a marketing ploy to attract talent. In short, we want to know that our mental health matters and we are not expected to burn out in the name of success.

Work is no longer just about paying the bills or adding to the bank account and being able to buy more things. That's not what makes us happy or healthy. It's also not what helps us become peak performers. But respecting and harnessing our human advantage to think, engage, and act with care absolutely is.

PAUSE ON THIS

- What do you care about?

  _____

  _____

- What matters to you in your daily life?

  _____

  _____

- What matters to you in the long run (purpose and goals)?

  _____

  _____

- What do you need to work better in your daily life?

  _____

  _____

- What do you need so that you can be healthy and happy while achieving your goals?

  _____

  _____

CHAPTER 7

Rethinking Habits

"We don't have to fit into our habits. Our habits have to fit us."

"I just need more willpower." "I just need to make myself do it." "Tomorrow I'll do it, but today I just have to...." This is the inner-dialog that many people feel stuck in. We beat ourselves up for not being disciplined enough, and of equal importance, we put ourselves on hold whenever something more urgent at work or at home pops up.

We live on habits. But it's important to consider whether or not they're working for or against us. Are they:

- helping us reach our goals?

- helping us work better every day?

- helping us live the kind of life we want?

- helping us forge the kind of relationships we want?

- supporting our well-being and cultivating work-life quality?

Knowing What We Need to Do Isn't Enough

When I began my career as an integrative nutrition and health coach, people would come to me with all sorts of reasons to create change in their lives ranging from wanting to lose weight, gain more energy, and feel stronger to wanting to better manage stress, be more focused and productive. At first, I thought that giving people the information about what their bodies needed and why it was good for them would be enough for them to change their habits. They asked me for the action steps; however, two weeks later, they'd come back with excuses for why it wasn't possible. Some would feel ashamed, guilty, and defeated, referring to themselves as "bad," "weak," or "failures."

Through these conversations, I realized that I wasn't helping anyone by telling them what to do, how to eat, or even why it mattered for their overall health, because knowing what to do is simply not enough or what creates change. After all, if it did, we'd all be healthy and rocking our lives by now.

We see this all the time, don't we? We make promises or resolutions and tell ourselves that tomorrow, or Monday, or next week, we'll start our new routine. Despite our best intentions though, it rarely works out the way we planned as honing new habits is not as simple as changing our wardrobe. New Year's Resolutions are a perfect example of this. At the beginning of the year, we sit down and create a list of the changes we want to make, goals we want to hit, and the new habits we want to have, yet by February, most people have already given up and resorted back to their old habits and patterns, operating as they have always done.

There's nothing wrong with you just because it's not easy to change your ways. It's our human nature to choose what's urgent before what matters and under stress, we choose to fix the problems we are facing instead of taking care of ourselves. That's the point here, to learn that we don't have to choose.

Seeing that telling people what to do didn't help anyone played a big role in why I began studying hypnotherapy. However, my goal wasn't to fix people's habits or instantly give them new ones when they came out of a trance. My focus was to understand how to make change accessible and possible and where our motivation comes from. Hypnotherapy is essentially about tapping into our core inner resources by "bypassing" the stories that keep us stuck and instead, focusing on our strengths and what we are capable of achieving.

I remember a young man who wanted to stop smoking, and even though that wasn't my lane, I agreed to help as I was already working with him on self-awareness and growth as he developed his real estate business. "I still have the urge to smoke," he said after a few weeks. "How much longer do you think till you fix me?" I paused and asked him what he meant by "fix me," and he replied, "to not want to smoke anymore." I realized what was happening and I asked him if he actually wanted to stop smoking. "No, of course not, I love it!" he said. "I know I *should* stop, so I want you to make me."

This is just one example of so many interactions I've had with people who believe they "should" do something before they've come to the point of truly wanting to make a change by first connecting with why it truly matters to them.

Disruption Is a Part of Life

I constantly hear from people, including leaders, that they don't feel in charge of their own calendar. We might have the best intentions to take a break during the day, eat lunch, and get everything on the to-do list done by 5 p.m.; however, it's rarely how the days play out, is it? Life and work tend to get in the way of our self-care, especially because we have been trained to see self-care as something separate from our responsibilities at work and our life in general. We also tend to build habits around needing a predictable schedule to make it work when our world and daily lives have become anything but predictable. But what if we accepted disruption as a normal part of life? What would change in the way we think about our habits if they are there to support us in dealing with our constantly changing and challenging reality?

When I was working in retail and running three stores, my job was to get things done and also to be available to help my teams solve problems. I quickly realized that even with the best planning, my days would never be predictable because problems have their own schedules. Then one day I also realized that the most important part of my job was to solve problems. Instead of feeling like I never had time to tackle my to-do list because of interruptions, I made it my job to expect problems to arise. It released so much of the stress I was feeling, because I could spend the time focusing on what my team needed to do their jobs and I made my to-do list something we executed together as a team.

That also meant that it was easier to respect breaks and pauses. Due to the constant public-facing nature of our customer-service-oriented jobs, we all needed to be able to step away and trust that someone else would take over. We saw ourselves as shared problem-solvers and therefore able to offer great customer service. We kept healthy boundaries together to make sure we were not on the sales-floor hangry or thirsty.

Once we all accepted the constantly changing nature of the day, we could set ourselves up to navigate change rather than feeling like it was a disruption to a so-called perfectly planned day.

To Change Our Habits, First We Need to Change the Way We Think

We tend to think that habits stand alone, but they don't. How we think and engage with the people around us, act, and respond to our environment at work are habitual patterns. Self-care is not just about wanting to work out and get healthy; it's about changing the way we live and work as whole human beings.

Habit researchers like Charles Duhigg and James Clear have written books about how we build and break our habits by understanding the cause and effect of the cue, response, and reward. Daniel Pink in his book *Drive* talks about motivation from a place of reward or punishment and our need for agency over our lives. Burnout is more about not having agency over our work and life than it is about the amount of time we are working. That goes for habits too. Reclaiming agency over our choices makes us feel more successful in harnessing change and why we need Power-Pausing to avoid getting triggered into automatic behaviors by cues. When we see and smell something, we are triggered into wanting it. Like Pavlov's dog studies in the 1940s, we humans are trained to crave. Once we have tasted something sweet and like it, just talking about it, seeing it, or smelling it, makes us want it.

When my dad was trying to quit smoking for example, he realized he craved a cigarette every time he picked up the phone—which was basically all day long. The phone call was his cue, his response was to grab a smoke and light up, and his reward was inhaling the smoke as it calmed him down.

As for me, when I used to arrive at my office, I'd go straight to the cupboard for a morning snack as I saw it as a way to chill out after my commute and get myself ready to see clients. Somewhere along the way, I'd convinced myself that I needed this snack to balance my blood sugar since I wouldn't have a break before lunch. I used to be hypoglycemic so it was just a left-over defense mechanism that I had not even paused to question.

All is not lost though. We can absolutely reclaim agency in our lives. This won't happen by avoiding the cue, however, but rather by taking the time to understand the triggers.

For example, a bakery opened across the street from my office, and they sold these delicious fruit tarts similar to the ones I used to love back home in Denmark. Three times a day, I'd walk by the bakery window and challenge myself not to buy one of those delicious treats. As a reward, sometimes on Fridays, I'd buy one and eat it alongside a cup of Earl Grey tea. But somehow it didn't do the trick, and I didn't feel satisfied. After pausing and asking myself what was really going on, I realized that it wasn't really the fruit tart that I wanted. It was my mom. The tart was the trigger that reminded me of the times we ate them when we went shopping together. Once I realized this, I no longer craved the fruit tart. I could look at them and smile because they are now the trigger to think of my mom with love.

Reclaiming Agency over Our Habits

The way we normally think about changing habits is to avoid the trigger completely or learn a new response that aligns with a new reward. Under stress though, that is ineffective. When times get tough, we put all of our intentions for new habits aside. We even forget we were supposed to do them, which leads to beating ourselves up and even saying, "Oh well, I already messed up so I might as well keep going!"

Whenever people tell me that it's the mindset that keeps getting them stuck, I ask what they do when they step in dog poop. This always elicits a funny look, but when I explain that this mindset is the equivalent of saying, "Dang, I just stepped in dog poop; let me keep stepping in it to get it all over both of my shoes!" they get the point.

The faster we can reclaim agency, the better we will navigate change and challenges, even when we feel under a great deal of stress. In order to reclaim agency over our patterns, habits, and choices though, we first need to pause. This simple act allows us to choose how to respond instead of rushing to react.

If we only focus on changing the actual habit we want to change, we will struggle to do so. However, if we focus on recognizing why we react the way we do and what we are trying to achieve—our true need—then we learn something about ourselves that helps us harness our choices.

After all, intention fuels attention and good things happen when we take the time to support ourselves when we need it most—right *now*.

Know Your Triggers

The patterns we have at work are similar to the habit loop described previously. We are triggered by something that happens in our day and we automatically react based on what we have always done to either avoid something painful or gain something pleasurable, which is the "reward" we have learned we will achieve by that reaction.

We are all emotional beings and our upbringings have given us a collection of memories that have created a pattern of how we deal with circumstances that we face every day. Memories are triggers, and circumstances might remind us of old feelings, some of which can be either painful or loving. It can be a smell, a sound, words, situations, and of course, people. Getting to know our triggers is how we reclaim agency. For example, I have had to get used to facing conflict in a constructive way because my memories of conflict meant my mom would sometimes stay in her room crying for three days after an argument. Learning to pause with the feelings that arise around conflict is not easy, but I can now choose how to face these conflicts instead of running away, as I did for years. The "reward" I was attached to was to ease the discomfort of conflict and my unconscious reaction and automatic habit had become to diffuse conflict by distracting myself, changing the subject, making a joke, or simply figuring out a way to leave the situation. As a small child, I would literally run away when in trouble and as the years passed, anger became my version of running away from the situation.

With self-awareness, we can learn to face these reactive behaviors so that we can instead choose the kind of change we want to cultivate. Diffusing discomfort with anger is not helpful nor healthy for anyone. As an adult and a leader, we need to learn to be comfortable with discomfort when triggered. It's essential to our well-being and that of others, to cultivate a healthy culture where we are able to navigate change and grow.

That said, when we are exposed to change and situations that pose a challenge, it is a natural human reaction to feel stressed and see this as a threat. Entering unfamiliar territory and facing uncertainty can trigger fear and that put us in survival mode because we don't know what we are supposed to do about it. Yet.

That's why it was so very stressful to figure out how to navigate COVID. The situation kept changing and we felt pretty powerless, not knowing what to expect. We started working from home, and as much as we might have thought that would be a nice break, it also added all kinds of other new challenges that we did not have to navigate before. Figuring out what COVID even was, whether or not we were going to get it, how it would affect us, the uncertainty around how long we might be in lockdown, working from home (if we were lucky enough to still have a job), home-schooling, and what to do about keeping family and ourselves safe, all of it at the same time added tension, which comes from the discomfort of change. Working from home, it didn't take long for the doubt to set in as to whether we were doing a good job, taking proper care of our kids, adjusting to tech fast enough, and whether or not we were coming across as a professional while balancing the computer on top of the laundry. We needed to completely rethink our way of operating, including the habits we used to rely on, and it hurt, didn't it?

We also needed new skills to learn how to engage with others so that our own FUD and stress did not negatively impact our conversations with others. We needed to learn how to connect, communicate, and collaborate in a way that fostered a sense of "I see you" even when we could only see our peers from the neck up over grainy Zoom calls, reminding people to unmute so we could hear each other. We will probably laugh at that one day.

We started asking questions about what we needed to make work *work* better for not only ourselves but also for our team members, and we stopped being so hard on ourselves for not being perfect. Whether or not we realized it though, we stopped "should-ing" ourselves and let things fall through the cracks for a moment. In a strange way it felt nice, didn't it? That's where The Self-Care Mindset® comes in handy. It provides a framework where we can pause, listen, set, and direct our intention, allowing us to think, engage, and act better.

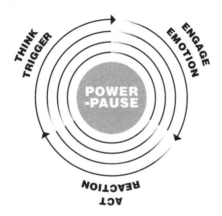

Source: Path For Life®

Our Choices Are Based on Fear or Desire

Understanding fear and desire is essential to learning to master our choices and how we make our habits work better for us so that they can support us in doing what matters right now. What's interesting about fear and desire is that they are not two opposite things. Desire comes from what we care about, which is the strongest drive we have as human beings, while fear comes from being afraid of losing what we care about.

The challenge here is to shift our attention away from what we are afraid of losing and focus instead on what we care about.

We react from a place of fear when we are stressed and afraid that we will not get our work done by the end of the day, especially if others are waiting for us to complete our tasks. In this scenario, we tend to drop everything else and even if we have good intentions to take care of ourselves, we push it off, telling ourselves that we can wait because work is more important. Sound familiar? This is when the survival-mode mindset kicks in, and we go on high alert. This often end up with us "should-ing" ourselves for having fallen into the "work first, self-care later" trap once again, when we get the time to look back on the day. It's okay if this hits close to home because that is what we humans do; we solve what's urgent first and tell ourselves we can wait. The thing is though, your best self can't wait.

When working with clients, I always ask why they want to learn how to take charge of their well-being. I also ask questions around what kind of change they'd like to make and the impact it could have as well as what "good" would look like for them. The questions are not just about their own personal well-being but also for the sake of their performance and how they imagine it would affect their work to have more energy and better focus. The key to change, though, is the core question: *"Why does that matter to you?"* If it's because they're scared of losing their job, it will not work because they would react from a FUD mindset and do what's urgent (work) and abandon their self-care (supporting themselves to work better) instead of a care-driven mindset, driven by what matters.

When we pause and ask the question, "Why does this matter?" we can make our priorities work better for us rather than against us, and we can face the triggers that we otherwise let direct our choices. At any moment you can pause and ask yourself, "Am I doing this because of what I want to avoid (fear), or am I doing this because of what I want (desire)."

To see the difference between being driven by fear or desire, let's look at a conversation I had with a past client. When she came to me, she was convinced that change wasn't possible for her because she had tried so many times before to create healthy habits and work always got in the way. After exploring both her fear and desire, it turned out the real reason why she wanted to change wasn't just for fear of her health falling apart, it was so that she could be in better shape and have energy left over after work to play with her grandchild. That's what she cared most about and ultimately that became the fuel to change her habits and improve her health.

Essentially, as humans we are designed to survive, and we have gotten a little stuck in thinking that self-care is the retreat and recovery from operating out of a place of survival, which is what many of our relationships with work look like. We work to survive—aka make money—to pay for shelter, food, and clothes, and in our modern work-style, the pace has also added the extra element of stress and performance as it becomes all about hustling. It all triggers the fear mindset and then we seek to recover from fear, which is how we end up with too much ice cream at night as we choose pleasure and give in to our desires. This seesaw way of living has created unhealthy habits of drinking coffee all day to "spark" our energy and then we relax our stress with overindulgence at night to stop our minds from rummaging over the worries that keep us stuck in FUD. A sign I saw in Greece put it best: "Lord give me coffee to change the things I can change and wine to accept what I can't."

Tapping into why something matters to us and what we care about is the foundation for learning to harness the power of self-care. Have patience; this is a process of unraveling old, learned behaviors and opening up to a new mindset that gives you the tools to harness your human advantage.

Please notice I did *not* say we are "only human" because I don't believe we are *only* human. I believe we're awesome and unique, and we don't need to fix ourselves. We need to understand ourselves and what drives us so we can support ourselves throughout the day to be our best selves, whatever that looks like right now. No "shoulds" needed.

PAUSE ON THIS

Use the following questions to observe and become more aware of your patterns that automatically become how you "fix" the discomfort instead of leaning into it.

- What are some of the "shoulds" that you tell yourself on a regular basis?

  _____

  _____

- What are the triggers at work?

  _____

  _____

- What are the triggers at home?

  _____

  _____

- What do you do when you are triggered?

  _____

  _____

CHAPTER 8

Self-Care Is a (Growth) Mindset

"The one thing in life that's for certain is change."

Change is part of life. We grow up just a little every day and we mature just a little every day. Seasons change and as the saying goes, "We cannot step into the same river twice because it has already changed." And so have we. Change is an interesting challenge for us humans.

If you're like most people, change is something you either resist, embrace, or pursue. It's a bit of a paradox as we want things to change, but we don't always want to change. The discomfort of change can hold some of us back as it triggers our insecurities and imposter syndrome, while for others, it's the excitement of change that makes up life. Change plays out in our relationship with evolution and triggers both our human fear and our human desire. On one hand, we might want change, crave change, and dream about change when our current situation is not optimal, while on the other hand, when we feel happy and content, we often want things to stay the same.

While change comes in numerous forms and flavors, at its core, there are three primary types. First, there's the type of change that happens unexpectedly that we didn't ask for. Second, there's the type of change that we want to make and need to figure out how to implement. Third, there's the type of change that's gradually happening around us, and it affects us in a more indirect way while giving us time to adjust.

Take a moment to pause and think about your relationship with change and how you normally respond to it.

- What's your first reaction when change happens to your schedule? Do you get agitated and stressed? Or do you let it roll off your shoulders and go with the flow?

- How do you feel and respond when someone tells you that something isn't working and you have to change? Do you get anxious or angry? Or do you become open-minded and curious?

- Think of a time when you wanted to change something and sit with how you felt in that moment. Did the change in front of you feel overwhelming? Or did it feel exciting?

- When changes are being implemented at work, do you feel resistance, fear, and anxiety? Or do you feel curiosity, confidence, and courage?

The challenge is that we humans like to know what's coming our way. However, the reality of life is that we often don't. This is not always easy to accept, but to not end up in survival mode when change comes knocking, we must learn to be more comfortable with not knowing. We must learn to pause and get curious and take the steps we need to bridge the gap between where we are now and where we are going. Without curiosity, that gap between now and the future can feel overwhelming and scary.

Imagine the distance between where you are now and where you are headed. Even if it is unknown, think of it as small steps and not a giant leap. For some people, change feels like standing on one side of a gap while seeing your goal on the other side. How will you build a bridge? For some it feels like it's around a corner and they cannot see what change will look like. What small steps can we take for now to feel we are getting closer?

The key to embrace change is to focus on what we hope to achieve and ask what we need to make it work. If we focus on the unknown as potential danger, we end up in survival mode, looking for what can go wrong; if we pause and stay curious about what's possible, we activate our ability to solve problems that occur along the way. The reality is once you've crossed the gap between what you know and where you ultimately end up, you can look back and see that you did it, and the process you went through taught you something, especially about yourself. This is also essential for building trust so that you can harness change in the future as it serves as a reminder of all the times you've done it in the past. But for many, when faced with change, we focus too much on the unknown, which can paralyze us.

Due to the discomfort we feel when moving past our comfort zone, we typically end up falling back into our old patterns that feel safe even when we know they aren't working for us. But at the same time, as human beings we have a knack for adjusting to change. Sure, it takes time and some getting used to, but this is the thing when change happens to us: we are incredibly adept at adapting.

Change is often seen as disruptive but it's important to remember that so is innovation. So what if we could learn how to use change in a more constructive and inclusive way by using Power-Pausing and asking questions, using curiosity and courage to get to the clarity that gives us the confidence to create? Yes, that's a lot of Cs for change. What do you need so that you can transform change into an opportunity?

Turning Change into Opportunity

Change is considered the most stressful aspect of our lives as it makes us question the trust we have within ourselves. It can come in the form of a divorce, illness, moving, or losing our jobs. Then there's the type of change that comes with the loss of a family member, partner, friend, or pet. My life has been rich with change. Or depending on how you look at it, marked by change. And most of the changes I've had to navigate in life were not by choice, but because of loss.

When I was 26 years old and had just arrived in the United States, I left behind my family, career, and everything I knew to follow my new husband to New York. I was deeply in love. However, with all the uncertainty of reestablishing myself in a new country and unable to find a job that matched the career I left behind, with each passing day, I became more and more depressed and began doubting the choices I had made. I felt like I'd made a mistake leaving a successful career, and I was overwhelmed being in a new country without a support system or network to help me navigate a new and completely unknown work environment. At the time, it felt like the loss of all of my hopes, dreams, plans, and most significantly, the loss of what I considered my identity.

What brought me out of that pothole, though, was asking myself questions that helped me reclaim my curiosity and courage. I kept asking questions to help navigate the unknown terrain in front of me so that I could stay open-minded and open-hearted rather than rushing toward and clinging to some safe harbor. As a result, I started graphic design and photography classes to reignite my creativity. It's worth noting though that this decision wasn't about undertaking a career in the arts; it was simply about studying something new that inspired me to think differently while also supporting my background in marketing and communication. It changed the trajectory of my career choices completely. I re-discovered my love for creative thinking and problem solving. I started working with Knoll, a contemporary design furniture company in the design development department and then with Vitra, where I ran marketing and public relations. Later I joined the creative agency of Peter Arnell and worked on developing retail concepts for fashion clients. This then lead me to opening my own creative design studio, which I ran for nine years. A trajectory that I could not have imagined this trajectory without the push from the change that happened because of moving to the United States and feeling lost.

With everything going on around us, I think many of us can relate to those feelings. On top of the turmoil the world is going through, many of us have also faced a major shift in the way we work since COVID came on the scene. We still don't know how our new work-life future is going to ultimately play out. This is scary. But it's important to recognize that change presents an opportunity to take the steps to reclaim more agency over our work-life quality and see this moment in time as an opportunity for growth and transformation.

Turning Discomfort into Comfort

No matter how we look at it, change is growth. Change is an ending of what we know and the beginning of what we learn. You can think of it this way: Change is the process of becoming comfortable with discomfort until the new becomes familiar. It's also how we reclaim agency.

When we face something new that's not welcome, discomfort takes over. We want to get rid of it, fix it, or suppress it. It happens all the time. It's part of our human behavior that automatically kicks in; it's the reaction rather than the mindful response that comes when we don't pause long enough to notice what's happening.

We often react to this by working harder and faster, while snacking and overeating and maybe even drinking a little too much. On the flip side, when we desire a certain change, since we like instant rewards and want to get them now because we expect they're going to improve our lives, we can end up making rushed decisions to cross the gap.

Both situations could use a Power-Pausing between the trigger and the reaction so that we can allow the discomfort to inform us and ask the questions that help us navigate change.

Change the Question, Change the Outcome

When we are under stress, we rush to solve the problem or we react based on what we have always done, using our 95 percent unconscious automatic behaviors, forgetting that we get stuck on repeat when we hang on to the safety of what we know.

To help us navigate change, it's important that we begin by focusing on the process of change rather than getting wrapped up in the end result. This way we can start plotting the map, getting the tools, and securing the steps we need to take.

A growth mindset is to stay open to new and relevant information while also learning to let go of what we know. Are you willing to *not* know for just a little longer instead of doing what feels safe and comfortable? Can you pause for just a little longer and ask more questions so that you can use the power of curiosity to make sure you solve the right problem and find new ways of solving old problems?

It's essential for all of us—whether we're in a creative/innovative field, production, customer service, or sales, or whether we're entrepreneurs or leaders—to learn how to harness change through curiosity so that we can grow.

The key to unlocking positive change is to use our "intention to fuel our attention" as it shifts us out of the "looking-for-answers-mindset" and into one where we begin asking ourselves, and each other, the questions that help us think better.

Using our intention to fuel our attention so that we ask ourselves better questions is a simple tool, but that doesn't mean it's easy. It's only human to want the answer that gets us all the way across the gap as quickly and pain-free as possible. As a result, we grab the first answer and run with it rather than continuing to ask ourselves questions to build the steps that safely gets us across. Simply put, pausing and asking ourselves one curious question after another is how we can build the clarity, courage, and confidence to change with more care and *purpose*.

What Do I Need Right Now So That I Can...?

The beauty of embracing the pause is it allows you to notice how you feel while opening the door to ask the simple, but powerful question when you are facing a challenge: *"What do I need right now so that I can...?"*

For example, let's put the power of this question into action by starting with a simple everyday challenge like feeling tired as you begin each day.

- Instead of asking yourself, "Why do I feel tired all the time?" change your question to, "What do I need so that I can have more energy?"

- Maybe you realize that you need more sleep, which opens the door for the question, "What do I need so that I can get more sleep?"

- Maybe you realize that you need to go to bed earlier, which leads to the question, "What do I need so that I can go to bed earlier?"

- Maybe you realize you need to stop watching TV so late into the night so you ask the question, "What do I need so that I can turn off the TV earlier?"

- Maybe you realize the answer is to go for a walk after dinner instead of crashing on the couch, which opens the doors for the question, "What do I need so that I can go for a walk after dinner?"

- Maybe you realize the answer is to recruit a friend to take evening walks with you.

This may sound basic but continuing to build with each question gives you the ability to create the path for change, a comfortable way forward one step at a time to get you across the gap.

You can use this same *"What do I need so that I can..."* formula of asking questions for everything you do. For example, maybe your intention is to have more confidence. As a result, instead of putting yourself in more of a hole by asking yourself why you lack confidence, you flip the script and focus your attention on asking yourself, "What do I need so that I can reclaim my confidence?" And with each "little-big" step that presents itself by asking yourself growth-minded questions, you walk your way gently, and firmly, toward your end goal.

Grow, Grow, Grow

I felt scared and overwhelmed when facing the unknown ahead of me when I lost my parents. I wasn't even sure I wanted to stay in the fashion industry even though the business I'd started while my dad was ill was doing well.

The day after he died, I walked to the park to go for a run just like I'd done every morning while caring for him. I still remember how scared I felt of the void that I knew was coming. My dad had always been my cheerleader and my "coach," and I felt as if I didn't know how I was going to find my way forward without his guidance.

Call it luck, fate, or simply being in the right place at the right time, but on the way to the park. I saw a sign in the window of a flower shop that I must have passed by a hundred times but hadn't taken the time to notice, and it stopped me in my tracks. It read: "Every blade of grass has an angel standing over it whispering grow, grow, grow!"

I don't know about you, but I love that.

When we pause and ask questions that focus on what we need, we can reclaim agency over the changes we are facing; we can harness the power of curiosity, clarity, and courage. To steal part of the line from the message I saw that day—"You can do it. Let yourself grow, grow, and grow through change."

PART II

Engage—The CARE Framework

CHAPTER 9

It's Who We Are That Makes Us Great

"It's not how hard we work or our titles that makes us great; it's our humanity that makes us great."

When I was a little girl, my dad told me a story about how he went to the king's castle in Copenhagen to install a new loud-speaker system. After he was done and showed the king how to use it, the king grabbed the microphone and started playing "Choo-choo-train." After a while, he turned to my dad with a big smile and said, "Wow, this makes me so happy, I don't have to wait for the echo to end so I can speak like a normal person now."

My dad would tell me stories like this to remind me that we are all human on the inside. It's not how hard we work or our titles that make us great; it's who we are that makes us great.

Since the industrial revolution, society as a whole has valued *doing* as the measure of performance, success, and identity. You see it when people lose a job they love because they lose their identity as well. You see it when people retire as many fall into a crisis of identity and no longer feel useful.

When my dad was dying, we spent five months in deep conversations going back over our lives together, and a pattern became very apparent: he touched people's lives. As word of his condition spread among the people he had worked with over the years as an executive search consultant, his inbox was flooded with messages about how much he had impacted people. But this wasn't because he had done something for them; it was because he had listened, asked questions, and simply given people space to discover what mattered to them.

This was a learning process for me. Through our conversations, it became obvious that what matters at the end is not money, titles, and status, but rather our human connections and the love and care we share because that's what we remember.

My dad admitted that he could have been more "successful" if he'd been willing to sacrifice more of his personal joy, but he wasn't. As for me, I realized that at that stage of my career, I'd done the opposite and sacrificed personal joy for society's definition of "success." I was working for the glamour of the industry I was in, and even though I'd reached certain heights, I didn't feel successful because the work I was doing had no meaning for me. I wasn't being of service or helping anyone live happier and healthier lives, which was the work I really cared about.

In the process of caregiving for my dad, he gave me the gift of opening my eyes to the fact that what drives us is what we care about.

Care in Action

While doing a residency a few years ago in Costa Rica, I interviewed different people working in the food business about passion. I wanted to understand what was driving them. I spoke with farmers, cooks at small, local restaurants, and chefs at upscale restaurants, and I met with their families. I asked them all the same questions: What are you passionate about? What drives you? What matters to you?

I heard stories from farmers about growing up on the farm and the importance of putting good food on the table for their families. Even though they weren't rich by society's standards, they were proud of their crop and they appreciated being part of a community of farmers, who all had each other's back. Many of them didn't have very much. They'd been given the land by the government to build a life for themselves, and they did so by sharing what they each grew. They cared about each other and they shared the efforts. If someone's house needed repair, they all came together. Being able to take care of their families and each other gave them joy. The "shared-care" mattered.

As for the high-end hotel and restaurant chefs and crews, it essentially came down to having a deep appreciation for the food they served and how it was received by their customers. The cooks told me how they would run to the window of the kitchen to see the joy on people's faces when they tasted the first bite. It wasn't status; it was the human joy that ignited their passion. They cared about the experience their customers cared about. The "shared-care" mattered here too.

Passion and Purpose

What I've consistently heard over the last two decades of my work is that people think having purpose means to do great things and make an impact. This may be true for some. However, we need to demystify purpose a bit here so that we can recognize that we use purpose all day long. Just like self-care, purpose is in the background of who we are, not what we do.

I hear stories of people feeling lost, confused, depressed, and angry because they aren't sure about what their life purpose is supposed to be. Of course, we know "What's my purpose?" is the big elusive question. We have the illusion that there's something wrong with us because just like self-care has been made into this "perfect life," so too has a purpose-led life. For many years, I searched for my purpose thinking I was going to find it outside of myself and some epiphany was going to hit me.

To the outside world, I probably look as if I have pursued and lived in alignment with my purpose for years. People see me as someone very focused and committed to changing the way we think about self-care so that it can work better for us. And I am. However, it wasn't an idea I came up with as this grand purpose. The experience of losing my parents taught me what I truly cared about, and it has continued to evolve since then.

Purpose is not a destination

Every day, what we care about directs our choices; we just don't see it when we are busy doing life. Every day, it's who we are that makes us unique and it's what we care about that drives us. And every day, our self-care is our connection that brings us back home to ourselves. You could say that our search for meaning is our search for ourselves and to understand ourselves better.

If we take a look at Maslow's hierarchy of needs, we have our need for physical safety at the bottom, then comes our need for psychological safety, then societal safety, and then we can self-actualize, which is at the top and what we strive toward. I can see why we think self-care is selfish; it's all about us reaching the top. But once we get there, we feel alone. I have consistently found that an inclusive work environment, where we feel seen and heard and where we can be ourselves and feel that we belong because of who we are is essential to our self-care.

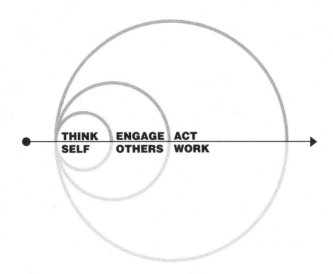

THINK   ENGAGE   ACT
SELF   OTHERS   WORK

If we don't feel like we matter and contribute at work, our self-worth is challenged. We bring this feeling home with us, which makes us feel like it doesn't matter if we take care of ourselves there either. Self, our relationship with others, and our work are completely interconnected because we are emotional beings. Whether we acknowledge it or not, we make choices based on how we feel, want to avoid feeling, and what we want to feel instead. How we feel is the underlying navigation system that drives us human beings, and that's why care matters.

The CARE Framework

I developed the CARE framework after years of working with people, and I realized that there are four areas that we need to focus on to get to know ourselves better: connect with what we care about and harness our self-care. These four areas include:

- Learning how our self-talk affects us and how we can change our inner dialog to help us grow.

- Learning to understand our own emotions and having the language and tools to cope and navigate how we feel.

- Learning to respect our own needs by taking responsibility for our choices and habits in a way that implements self-care into our daily lives.

- Learning how to speak up so that our needs are met and healthy boundaries are kept.

The CARE framework is rooted in asking ourselves better questions because as you might remember, *how* we ask questions directs our attention, helps us get unstuck, and find our way forward.

The CARE framework is based on four questions:

- **Self-Communication:** *"Who's thinking, who's talking? Am I my inner critic or my inner coach right now?"* This allows us to cultivate curiosity, clarity, and courage.

- **Self-Awareness:** *"How am I in there right now?"* This allows us to embrace mindfulness to acknowledge how we feel, which opens the door for us to be more aware, adaptable, and agile.

- **Self-Responsibility:** *"What do I need so that I can?"* This allows us to cultivate daily habits that support and promote peak performance built on respect and resilience from the inside out.

- **Self-Expression:** *"How do I ask for what I need?"* This allows us to communicate healthy boundaries and expectations and ask for what we need to foster empathy, equity, and feel empowered within ourselves.

The next four chapters will be about learning the tools to integrate The Self-Care Mindset® into our daily lives because self-care is not a side-hustle; it's how we grow and change, harness our well-being, and reclaim work-life quality.

As we embark on this next part of the book, remember: Self-care is not the goal itself; it's how we reach our goals.

THE SELF-CARE MINDSET®

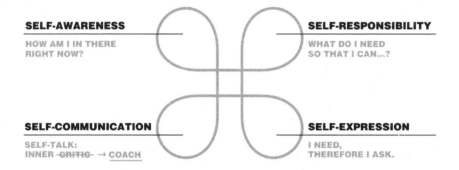

SELF-AWARENESS

HOW AM I IN THERE
RIGHT NOW?

SELF-RESPONSIBILITY

WHAT DO I NEED
SO THAT I CAN...?

SELF-COMMUNICATION

SELF-TALK:
INNER ~~CRITIC~~ → COACH

SELF-EXPRESSION

I NEED,
THEREFORE I ASK.

CHAPTER 10

Self-Communication

"Who's thinking, who's talking? Am I my inner critic or my inner coach right now?"

My mom grew up believing she was a mistake. She told me the story of how she was born an illegitimate child, at least that's what you would call someone like her in 1936, when my grandmother was a young woman who got pregnant without being married. According to my mother, she was a "Saturday night gone wrong." My grandmother was sent away to give birth in shame and my mother was then taken in by my great-grandfather (the blacksmith), to be raised in the town where my grandmother's 12 other siblings lived. Yes, all 13 siblings lived in the same town. My mom grew up as the black sheep, rarely seeing her mother, my grandmother, who was away at school to become a hairdresser.

In addition to my mom telling me stories about how she wasn't included in birthday parties and ate cake alone in the bathroom, she shared how my grandmother blamed her for never becoming a well-known opera singer because getting pregnant ruined her life.

My mom struggled with feeling unwanted and unworthy of love. It affected her relationship with both me and my dad. Of course, being bipolar added to her emotional struggle and the turmoil of my upbringing. I asked her once if she was ever happy and she replied, "Not very often, and not for very long at a time."

She was completely stuck in the inner dialog of not being good enough and feeling like she didn't fit in or belonged. Her life was all about what she was *not*. She never knew who her biological father was and never tried to find out. She felt betrayed from the get-go. When my grandmother met and married a young man who said, "Of course your daughter will live with us," my mom opened her heart to him, never saw anyone else as her dad, and he became the loving grandfather I got to know.

If you were to ask anyone else, my mom was loving, kind, funny, beautiful, caring, and always ready to give a helping hand. At her funeral, the flowers filled the church, were lined up all the way down the aisle, and almost out the door. The church was full of neighbors, friends, family, and some people I didn't even know she knew. She was loved. She was wanted. She just never felt that way because the story of the inner critic had grabbed hold of her and she was never able to break free.

After my mom died from her third bout with breast cancer, I was talking to my grandmother about my mother's illness. "I hope it's not my fault that she got sick," she said. I wasn't sure if she meant the breast cancer, which she had twice herself, or the depression, which she also struggled with. I mentioned how my mother had a difficult upbringing and it probably wasn't helpful that she was, well, "a mistake and unwanted."

My grandmother looked at me in shock. "What are you talking about?" she asked. "I loved your mother. I begged to keep my little daughter instead of giving her up for adoption as I was supposed to do after I was sent away to give birth. I wanted to marry the man who got me pregnant as we loved each other, but we weren't allowed to because I was too young. Instead he was driven out of town by your great-grandfather. Your mom was the love of my life and everyone in town adored her. All my siblings, including your great-grandfather, spoiled her and every weekend I traveled back home to spend time with her. She was a love-child. And it was not your mom's fault I didn't rise to the stars as an opera singer. I had opportunities that I didn't take."

We both cried. I cried because I learned that my mom wasn't a mistake but rather a love story that was never told and my grandmother cried because the two of them never spoke about it, and now it was too late.

Looking back, it was the sad reality of what happens when we don't challenge the story of the inner critic and never pause to ask questions. Even if they are uncomfortable and scary, they may be what we need to break free from the inner dialog that keeps us trapped in the very box we don't want to live in.

To this day, I still wonder how my mom would have lived her life differently had she known she was loved and wanted.

What's the Inner Critic?

Though my mom's experience was unique to her and her alone, the inner critic shows up in many of us. We beat ourselves up for not being good enough and say things like, "There's something wrong with me!" "Why am I so stupid that I can't get it right?" The point isn't to get rid of the inner critic, but rather to make friends with it to transform it into the inner coach so that we can move more confidently toward growth, change, and peak performance.

We often judge people from what we see on the outside, not realizing the constant dialog going on inside all of us and the emotional turmoil that consumes many of us. Even in our sleep, the subconscious mind keeps working either for us or against us, depending on the questions we ask ourselves.

Remember the pothole from Chapter 3 and how when we are under stress, we focus on what's not working? That's the inner critic right there; we feel scared and worried that we aren't good enough, fast enough, capable enough, or friendly enough. We get stuck in the pothole. And rather than focusing on where we want to go, we ask questions that keep us paralyzed in this "not good enough" state, and it's wearing us out.

We often assume that change and growth are things we can just figure out. But at the same time, they can feel scary and we can easily fall into the inner-critic trap where we tear ourselves a new one over and over again. This is when Power-Pausing and hearing how our inner critic is thinking and talking comes in handy. It allows us to listen with a bit more self-compassion and care so we stay curious and find more clarity about what we need so we can become more comfortable with the uncomfortable. Or,, I can say it in another way—it's stressful to change and grow without the tools to do so with care.

We all have some version of the inner critic, don't we? It mainly shows up as the "I should have. . ." "I could have. . ." and "I would have. . ." thoughts we have after a long day. We begin to rehash what went wrong and start blaming ourselves for not being on top of things.

A great example of this happened in a keynote I gave about The Self-Care Mindset® to a group of young leaders. We were discussing how the inner dialog can feel like a harsh critic who will never let you win but pretends that's what it wants for you, therefore pushing you to work harder by being that critical inner judge. I asked them to write down some of the most critical ways they spoke to themselves. This made them laugh a bit because they each recognized the perfectionist inside of them even though some also thought the inner critic was an excellent way to drive them to achieve.

I then asked them to pair up and face each other, and as they were still laughing, I asked them to say the exact words they told themselves to the person in front of them. It didn't come as a surprise to me that they all refused. That was the point, to recognize how hard we are on ourselves and how we would not be that hard on someone else. Instead, we would cheer each other on to transform that inner critic into the inner coach, wouldn't we?

"I'm Not Good Enough!"

After the bullying I experienced in school, I always felt the need to be better, more interesting, wear better clothes, and look perfect. At work, my motivation was a constant drive for peak performance, fancy titles, and money. I probably don't need to tell you, but this didn't do me an ounce of good. I know I'm not alone in feeling this way. Many of my clients tell me that they believe they need to be hard on themselves to achieve their goals. We become people-pleasers to try to make everyone happy and like us; we become flexible to accommodate other people's needs. We agree to things we wouldn't normally agree with, and we overstep our own boundaries. And despite this, we still don't feel good enough, do we?

We might be in a meeting with people we think know more than we do, have higher positions, or feel like other people are being heard and we aren't. We might be in a relationship with someone we adore and we are scared that we are not enough and we might lose them. We might be among friends, but someone always has more, knows more, or has done more. When we compare ourselves to others, we fall into the trap of not being good enough, and we think we have to do more to compensate. As a result, we overdo, over-work, over-perform, and we keep doing all of these things over and over without rest. The inner dialog is consistently beating us up as we go through our days on the "more, more, more" rollercoaster of the inner critic hoping that one day we will be enough, we will be perfect, we will belong, and we will be someone others care about. Maybe you know this inner dialog too?

There are two sides to this. First, we need to recognize when the inner critic is in charge. Second, we need to recognize that we will never be enough to others if we don't feel enough within ourselves. After all, it's who we are that makes us great. And instead of having judgment of ourselves, we need some healthy self-compassion.

"I Am" Versus "I Feel"

There's a very big difference between the inner critic saying, "I am not good enough," and our self-caring, self-compassionate self saying, "I don't feel good enough right now." Pause on that a bit and say these two sentences to yourself: "I am not good enough," and "I don't feel good enough, right now." Does it feel different to you and in your body? Do you feel the energy change? Do you feel lighter when saying the latter?

Saying "I feel right now" lifts the burden, doesn't it? If not, sit with it a bit longer and say it again more slowly. Pause, breathe, listen, and feel the difference of the weight of the words.

When we say, "I feel that I'm not good enough right now," we can start to be more curious about ourselves and the circumstances we are in. It allows us to start asking questions and we begin to wonder what it is about the situation that makes us feel like we aren't measuring up right now. We can ask questions like, "What do I need so I can feel more confident?" This opens the door for us to be more curious as to whether it's because we are simply tired or if we need new skills. We can be curious if we are stuck in a conversation where we don't have enough information and we need the courage to speak up and say, "I don't know about that, and I will go learn more so we can continue this conversation later."

When we say, "I *am*," it becomes an identity, it becomes a box that defines us, and ultimately, it becomes a burden. When we say, "I *feel* right now," though, it becomes a feeling that is just there in the moment and does not represent who we are as a whole. I know this because many people over the years have come to me and said, "I don't matter!" "I am not good enough!"

Even if we don't feel like it all the time, we are all good enough. This feeling of not stacking up comes from comparing ourselves to others in what we do, how we perform, and what we achieve. What we can do instead, however, is tap into what we care about and ask what we need to live from the heart as it's the key to unlocking what truly drives us and achieve what truly matters to us.

As an example, following are a few simple switches in language that can make a big difference in being more self-compassionate.

- Instead of saying, "I'm stupid!" consider saying, "I feel stupid right now."

- Instead of saying, "I'm not smart enough," consider saying, "I don't feel capable of figuring this out with the information I have right now."

- Instead of saying, "I'm a bad person!" consider saying, "I feel I wasn't at my best in how I reacted right now."

- Instead of saying, "I'm a lost cause!" consider saying, "I feel stuck right now."

- Instead of saying, "I can't do anything on my own!" consider saying, "I need help to move forward right now."

To Listen or Not to Listen

When we are at war with our inner critic, we react instead of using it to ask more questions about what we need so that we can move beyond the inner voice that is telling us to stay where we are. It takes a lot more energy both physically, emotionally, and mentally to move beyond our comfort zone because it triggers that innate question and sense of "Am I safe?" This is why we get sweaty palms and heart palpitations when we do something outside what we normally do. It's why we get a strange feeling in our stomach. And it's why we might decide to agree with the inner critic rather than using it as information to move from fear to excitement in new environments. Simply put, asking questions allows us to move from critical to curious and ultimately, courageous.

To see this last point in action, let's look at how I approached my first leadership job. I was young, and I was tasked with heading up the lingerie and bathing suit areas in a department store in Denmark. At the time, I was instructed to get rid of "the old salespeople" and spruce things up a bit. Despite what was expected of me, I started out by asking the women who'd been there a long time what they thought needed to change to better meet customers' needs. Even though some of them didn't initially know, it became clear that by simply asking them their opinion, they indeed had opinions—they'd just never been asked before.

On top of this, I also asked them to sit in on my buying meetings and asked them how much of each item they thought they could sell. We met on a daily basis to see how their customer interactions were going and what we could learn from that. By letting them know that we needed each other and we each brought unique skills to the table, they responded to the challenge. My trust in them gave them the sense of being good enough. Together, we doubled the sales in just three months.

Had I walked in there without being aware of my inner critic, I would have been reactive based on my feeling "not experienced enough," which would have led me to hide my insecurities and try to prove myself. I would not have been curious, and we would not have been able to communicate and grow the department the way we did. We spruced up the place and "the old salespeople" stayed because they got their spark back.

Turn Your Inner Critic into Your Inner Coach

There's a Cherokee legend about a grandfather teaching his grandson about life. He tells him about the battle between two wolves, which resembles the war inside each of us. One of the wolves is angry, greedy, arrogant, and uses guilt and shame to control the other wolves. The other wolf, however, is kind, generous, and compassionate. The grandson pauses for a moment after hearing the story and then asks his grandfather which wolf will win to which the elderly man replies, "The one you feed."

Inside each of us, we have an inner critic and an inner coach. Which one we listen to is a decision we must constantly make, and it's essential that we do so with care. To begin to feed the right wolf, and ultimately, transform our inner critic into our inner coach, we can use a three-step process:

- Pause and take a couple of breaths while bringing your attention into your belly as you inhale, and as you let go of the breath, focus on the exhale to ground, and center yourself in your body.

- Listen to yourself to notice how you are thinking. Is your inner narrator being critical or curious? Are you asking "why not" questions? Are you being hard on yourself? Be honest with yourself even if you are trying to convince yourself it's for your own good.

- Ask yourself: "What would my inner coach say to help me align with why this matters to me?" Remember, we are not looking for the big purpose here, just the little ones that get you through the day as a whole human.

Here are some examples of feeding the good wolf, using the inner critic to inform the inner coach.

- **Inner critic:** "I'm not good enough to get this job."

- **Inner coach:** "It's okay that I feel concerned when trying something new. What do I need to know more about so that I can feel more confident about my skills and talents being right for this job?"

- **Inner critic:** "Why am I not able to get this done? It's so simple; I'm just too stupid."

- **Inner coach:** "I feel stuck right now. What do I need so that I can gain more insight and a new perspective?"

- **Inner critic:** "Why am I never the one getting chosen? Why do I never get to be part of the good team?"

- **Inner coach:** "I feel I'm not getting the attention I deserve. What do I need so that I can show up in a way that makes my manager see my possibilities?"

Looking at the previous list, you can see that "What do I need so that I can..." is embedded into the last part of the equation as it plays a starring role in the inner coach addressing what you need right now to achieve what you are hoping to accomplish.

You also see how we can play with the questions and shift our focus from the inner critic to the inner coach simply by pausing, listening to what's going on, and using that as information to change the question to ultimately, change the outcome. For example, saying to yourself, "I'm not strong enough!" is very different from saying, "I don't feel strong enough right now. What do I need so that I can build more strength and achieve a position on the team?"

Growing Pains

When we compare ourselves with others, we can end up struggling to feel good enough. It's important to remember though, that we can also use the comparison as inspiration for something we would like to change and use it as fuel for growth. For example, I always thought my legs were too short and my nose too big. I will never get longer legs but I could get a smaller nose if that really was important. Instead, I can build on the strengths that I do have and where I see others excel: I can absolutely build new skills, learn new ways of interacting, and I can support myself in what I need to be more comfortable with discomfort, when comparison triggers me.

Many of us feel like we need to fix ourselves. But we are not broken, so there's nothing to fix. What we need is to discover ourselves. In order to grow, we need to build new ways of thinking by pausing and listening to ourselves and build on our strengths. Practice asking yourself questions that unlock constructive thinking, and when you find yourself falling back into the old inner dialog, acknowledge yourself for catching it. The new language we develop when we change our inner critic to our inner coach is key as it allows us to create change by making new choices that work better for us so we can get to where we want to go.

As a quick but important aside, please don't expect to master this right away. It takes mindfulness to change something that has been automatic for a long time.

The inner critic is the comfort zone we have been living in for far too long, whereas the inner coach is uncomfortable because we have to face some truths with ourselves, and that's okay. You are right where you need to be if you are feeling some growing pains. Sometimes we must let go of what we have to get what we want.

PAUSE ON THIS

- What are some stories you consistently tell yourself that keep you stuck in your inner critic? Even though the story may be true, you can change your experience of the story or choose to ask the inner coach to help you rethink what you do with that story and use it as a springboard to get unstuck.

_____

_____

(continued)

(continued)

- What are some situations both at work and when you're with family and friends that typically trigger your inner critic?

  _____

  _____

- Lastly, think about the "I am" statements you say to yourself and consider how you could move them to a place of more self-compassion by using the "I feel right now" technique.

  _____

  _____

CHAPTER 11

Self-Awareness

"How am I in there right now?"

"It feels like ants inside." That's what my dad said to the doctor when we went in for a check-up after being in remission for a couple of months. "I think the cancer is growing again; it feels like ants inside." The doctor smiled with a look of confusion and dismissal, and with a small hint of laughter in his voice replied, "That's probably not the case, but we can take a scan if you'd like?" When he came back to tell us that the cancer was indeed growing again, he apologized for rejecting the notion that my dad could feel it as he'd never met anyone with such an awareness of that *felt sense* inside.

When most people think of self-awareness, they either connect it to career pursuits like knowing what they're good at, passionate about, or where they have limitations. But one aspect of self-awareness that's often overlooked is taking the time to heighten our whole body awareness from the inside out.

Many of the people I've met over the years in coaching have become numb to their body awareness because their relationship with their body is often not very kind, or at least, not very curious. The relationship falls somewhere between body-shaming and anger because we often feel that our bodies aren't living up to our—or society's—expectations. The reality is that we need our body to take care of us as much as our body needs us to take care of it. We must learn to work as a team with our bodies.

But when's the last time you asked yourself, "How am I in there?" where you paused to listen and have a conversation with yourself that was curious and kind?

Becoming more bodily self-aware in a "productive way" is something to get used to. In the beginning, it's like walking around in a new area you don't know yet. You just start looking and observing, not sure what to expect; you only know that you are going in a specific direction because that's what the map says. In today's world, we're using different devices to check in with our bodies to get a sense of what's going on inside, like monitoring our blood pressure and oxygen levels. These apps and tools can be helpful; however, there's more to it. We need to change the relationship we have with ourselves so that we can become a team with our own body and mind, using our awareness to become more adaptable and agile in the moment rather than waiting till the day is over to recover.

A good way to start is by taking better note of simple daily needs like thirst and hunger. Even though we have all been drinking water and eating food since we were toddlers, most people have not learned to be aware of their own body's signals and how to trust them. If you think back, you might have felt hungry as a kid and been told that you weren't because it wasn't dinner time yet and you just had a snack. Or you might have felt full and been told you can't be because you have food left on your plate and the allotted portion is barely touched. As much as our parents are well-meaning and trying to teach their kids to have a pattern and essential lifestyle habits, it sends messages to ignore our signals and NOT listen to our bodies. I often hear people say they don't feel hungry during the day only to overeat at night because they're starving.

This lack of appetite during the day is due to stress and cortisol suppressing hunger signals. When we relax, the hormones that regulate satiety shut off in an effort to make sure we don't starve, triggering us to binge. On a positive note, we humans are brilliantly designed for survival. The problem is that we shouldn't think of a workday as something we have to survive. We tend to call this emotional eating; however, I call it "stress eating" to avoid the shaming that comes along with it. Instead, let's focus on understanding the complex nature of how our bodies function and reclaim the connection we need to have with ourselves, our bodies, and our self-care to be healthy. People search online for answers regarding how to eat, when instead, we can learn to notice how we feel when eating and digesting food. As a result of doing that, we can create a way of eating that works for us to help us each know what we need to perform at our best.

And then there's awareness of our physical well-being all day long and how we keep the blood-flow and circulation going to support optimal energy and focus. I have lower back problems from scoliosis and years of gymnastics. Add in an Aikido throw gone wrong and a yoga injury, and I must be continuously aware of my posture. How I sit, stand, strengthen, and stretch my hips and lower back is how I use some of my Power-Pausing throughout the day. To keep headaches at bay I need to stay hydrated and keep my neck and shoulders moving too. Without some constructive body-awareness, I can find myself getting irritable, unfocused, and unmotivated, only to realize I have been sitting for too long and my mental energy is stuck in my stagnant body.

If I don't pay attention, check in, and do what my body needs me to do, I can end up with a couple of days of pain. That's not only annoying but also costing me my overall well-being, and with that, my productivity and effectiveness because I'm less mobile and distracted by the pain. You have probably felt the same, and unfortunately, we accept the discomfort more willingly than is good for us rather than pausing to learn to listen better to our bodies and what they need to stay in good functioning shape.

The Body on Stress

After my dad died, I went to yoga for the first time in ages. Halfway through the session, I realized I wasn't breathing. Well, I was breathing but little, shallow, tight breaths instead of rich and deep inhales and exhales. I'd been listening so intensely to my dad's breath for months to be in touch with how he was doing that I'd forgotten to use my breath to be in touch with how I was doing.

Pause for a moment and check in with how stress feels in your body. Do you feel tense? Do you get the feeling of blood rushing either to your head or away from it? Do you have tightness in your stomach? Are your shoulders in a knot and your lower back so stiff it feels like you are 30 years older than you are?

This is because when we are under stress we hold our breath and tighten our muscles. Even just being aware of this can help us to get up to move and stretch a bit between meetings and tasks. We need to maintain blood flow and circulation to sustain the energy in our bodies and be able to think clearly. Self-care at work is not about staying fit but understanding how much our mind relies on the body to maintain attention and focus. To stay engaged, we need to release tension and open up our circulatory system at intervals throughout the day. A French study some years ago showed the connection between sitting upright instead of slouching to maintain energy and how moving the spine impacts our ability to pay attention, hence why office chairs are more ergonomic now. So please don't think of something like getting up to take a walk as a waste of time because, in reality, it boosts our ability to spend time better.

We need to move the body to move our emotions too. When we are stressed, we tighten up. As a result, it can feel like fear and anxiety is taking over. If you struggle with anxiety, you already know how it feels for you. It can make you feel dizzy, as if all the blood is leaving your body or rising to your head as if you are on fire. That the world around you is either speeding up or slowing down. That everyone is watching you and you feel like an imposter. And you probably know how an anxiety attack impacts your breathing, to the point of a knife penetrating your chest. Anxiety is more intense than being stressed.

If we can help the body release some of the tension as it rises, we can also support ourselves in managing the buildup. The earlier we start noticing that we are holding our breath when we are overly focused or scared, the sooner we can begin to focus on improving our ability to breathe, reset our thoughts, and reclaim a sense of agency. This is just one of the ways being aware of how we feel in our bodies can help us navigate stress, soothe anxiety, and feel better throughout the day.

We recognize stress in our bodies in any number of ways from experiencing headaches, muscle tension, clenching, low libido, and difficulty sleeping. It shows up in our mood through irritability and anger, lack of focus and motivation, forgetfulness, restlessness, impatience, sadness, depression, and feeling anxious and/or overwhelmed. When we experience these feelings, it affects our behaviors and may be found in drinking too much coffee or alcohol, eating too fast, too much, or not at all, lack of or excessive exercise, not being able to sit still and overall erratic (maybe even aggressive) behavior, and social withdrawal.

If these feelings and behaviors hit close to home, taking time for consistent body scans can help to identify feelings and thoughts that aren't serving you.

How to Get Body-Scanning to Work for You

PAUSE and bring your attention to your breath, breathing in through your nose and out through your mouth. Breathe deep into your belly and allow it to expand when you inhale before letting go on the exhale, as if you are slowly blowing smoke out of your mouth. Have the intention to deepen each inhale into your belly to feel even more grounded before slowly exhaling. You can practice inhaling for four counts and exhaling for seven counts and notice if it helps you feel like you are sinking deeper and deeper into a state of relaxing your nervous system.

To continue, bring your attention to your feet, and simply notice how they feel. Are your feet buzzing, warm, cold, or are they feeling like they are lighter or heavier as you pay attention to them? You can practice shifting your attention by noticing one foot at a time.

Try to wiggle your toes, rotate your ankles, and simply notice what they feel like. For example, does it feel tight or smooth? Keep going up the lower legs, are your calves feeling tight, relaxed, weak, strong, tired, or maybe there's a sense of impatience in your legs? You can stop whenever you want and spend more time there.

Move up to the knees and notice any pain or tightness or if they feel ready to bend and stretch for you. Move up to your hips, notice, listen, and feel into them in that same curious attention kind of way and simply ask your body as you go, "How are you in there?" Stay with the physical aspect for this first body scan. If you want to check in more energetically, notice if there's a color or temperature in the body. Is it hot or cold, damp or dry? Or if there's an energy that feels dense or light, like a mist, fog, or smoke. There's no right way to communicate with your body; that's up to you to allow it to evolve by pausing, listening, and asking yourself with curiosity: "How am I in there right now?"

When you scan your body, it's important to have an attitude of curiosity about what you need to feel supported in getting through the day. It's not about judging your body for what it is—or what it is not—as we all know we probably go there enough.

If you're accustomed to your self-talk being overly critical, this type of curious dialog may feel strange at first. But keep at it. It's a great tool to ensure you and your body can get through the day more optimally.

A Morning Routine

Every morning, just after waking up and while still in bed, I spend a couple of minutes scanning, noticing, and listening to my body and my "self" to see how I'm feeling. I start by asking myself a group of simple questions that allow me to determine what I need to best face the day,:

- **Am I stiff and sore?** Do I need to stretch, do yoga, walk, or take a hot shower? Or do I need to be gentle because my body needs rest?

- **Am I anxious or excited?** Anxiety and excitement are the same feeling but different thoughts based on either fear or desire. Trying to calm down with meditation does not work at this time. At least it doesn't for most people. When feeling anxious, we tend to need to move and focus on how we can reclaim a sense of control and confidence. So rather than calming down, check in with yourself to get clarity on what works for you. Sometimes I need to reach out to someone to talk about my concerns, and I specifically ask them to just listen for where I'm stuck on something that I cannot control because I'm future-casting. Basically, I ask for help identifying the story that's keeping me stuck in anxiety over something I cannot control, fix, or change, and I need to reclaim my confidence and trust in myself.

- **Am I feeling happy or sad?** Our moods change, and it's just the way it is; no shoulds or judgment about it, notice and ask. If I'm sad, I tend to need to connect with other people and not feel alone, which is normally where my sadness comes from. I have learned through years of working with people who struggle with depression and loneliness that it doesn't come from being alone; it comes from feeling that no one cares or thinks about us. When I'm happy, it's often the same thing because I want to share what I'm happy about.

- **Am I waking up scared?** My dreams often affect me and so does what I ate the night before, or a movie I saw, and I often wake up feeling scared for no apparent reason. It's something that I have gotten used to, and I basically tell myself it's okay to be scared and remind myself that I'm okay and safe. I also ask myself what I might need to pay attention to that I'm not being mindful about. I intentionally use my fears to question myself if I'm focusing on what truly matters.

- **Am I feeling motivated or not**? We don't wake up motivated, but some days more than others we just feel more excited to do something.

I then always stretch in bed before I get up. I call it "bedercise." I lift my legs straight up in the air, roll my ankles, then fold my legs and stretch my lower back at a couple of different angles. Then I work on my core. I do some elbow-to-knee crunches and then I go to the side of my bed and do bed dips (also called bench dips) and some high push-ups. It all takes about 5–10 minutes, and I feel more ready for the day as I've gotten my body activated and warmed up. Since I do it daily, I'm keeping my core strength so even if I miss a day or two of yoga, it's no big deal as I can get right back to it. The best part is I can do this simple circuit when traveling as well.

Then I drink a huge glass of water, visit the bathroom, and then my dog Maya and I get outside for a little morning walk. Her breakfast, my tea, and then things depend on my schedule and what my work schedule is that day. It's the small stuff that creates consistency.

Being "Self-Conscious" Versus Being "Conscious"

I was facilitating a meeting with women executives when one of them mentioned how angry she was at her body for feeling rundown. Her comment allowed us to pause and recognize how easy it is to fall into the trap of judging our bodies for not being able to keep up with us or being good-looking enough. Unfortunately, society shouts non-stop the benefits of diets and images of what "being fit" is supposed to look like, which more times than not are men with chiseled abs, models wearing slinky outfits, and always having perfect nails. I get it. We sell ideas, ideals, and goals. However, we are also creating a misrepresentation of what's possible (or even healthy) for most of us, especially when being fit is not our job, but rather something we are trying to fit into our lives alongside everything else.

When we are self-conscious, we're measuring ourselves against expectations, which might make us feel awkward, unsure, uncomfortable, or embarrassed. We can either be judgmental about ourselves for these feelings, or we can choose to be conscious about feeling that way. The latter opens the door for us to choose to respond with self-compassion.

A client once told me how she would go through her entire closet every morning to find something to wear because all of it was "wrong." She felt so self-conscious at work that she couldn't think about anything else as she imagined everyone judging her outfit and her body shape. I jumped behind my chair, which had a tall back and I asked her, "What am I wearing?" Even though she'd been sitting across from me for 30 minutes, she couldn't recall my outfit.

We might feel like everyone is looking at us, but the reality is that people are more concerned about themselves. I'm not dismissing that many people feel judged by what they wear, and it's an issue of equity in the workplace as well. But I hope we can get to a place where we don't judge ourselves or each other, and we can harness our self-care mindset in such a way that we are not affected by it when it happens.

Social anxiety and self-consciousness versus self-awareness are essential to understand too. I often come across as confident when I walk into a room, and at this stage of my life, I am comfortable with who I am. But that was not always the case. Remember I told you earlier how I felt unwanted, like an outsider, and that when I was growing up I felt like I didn't belong? Well, for many years, I felt like a piece of furniture if no one spoke with me, and I was left to just take up space standing in a room. This was partly left over feelings from being bullied and teased in school for my pants being too short. I was super self-conscious and started measuring and comparing myself to others, wondering if I wore the right outfit and aware that I was not one of the pretty girls with a small nose. Yes, I was also teased for my big nose, and it even landed me in a beauty makeover spread in *Oprah* magazine. Side-note: I have learned to love my big nose. I cried over it when I was younger and asked if I could please get it fixed. But my dad convinced me to keep it, saying that it was pretty perfectly shaped and some of the most powerful, wealthy, and beautiful women in the world also had big noses.

Being self-conscious, we are stuck in the story we are telling ourselves about how we are not good enough, allowing that inner critic to take over. Being conscious, however, we can use our self-awareness to choose how we want to respond and embrace our inner coach.

PAUSE ON THIS

Scan your body from the inside out, not outside in. Avoid scanning how you look and instead notice how you feel to get a solid gauge on the ever-important question, "How am I in there right now?"

On a scale from 1–10:

_____

_____

- Do you feel tired or energized?

_____

_____

- Do you feel tightness or open and relaxed?

_____

_____

- Do you feel weakness or strength?

_____

_____

(continued)

(continued)

- Do you feel ready to start your day?

  _____

  _____

- Do you feel ready to get into your next meeting?

  _____

  _____

- Do you feel ready to do whatever is next ahead of you?

  _____

  _____

Emotional Self-Awareness

As humans, we are emotional beings and we carry these emotions around with us all day long. They flow through us and affect how we think and behave. We have many emotions and they vary based on what's going on. Our basic emotions that we tend to judge as negative are sad, mad, and scared. We think of the positive ones as joy, surprise, and anticipation/excitement. If you explore the nuances, you can fine-tune each of these core groups into even more emotions (some say there are 28). Even though I don't believe it's important to label our emotions to reclaim agency, I do believe we must develop the self-awareness to understand how we feel.

When one of my clients was anxious, overwhelmed, and scared about what the future might hold, I asked her to pause and listen inside for a moment and describe how she felt, not with the emotional labels that we use to make sense of how we feel, but by describing that felt sense that is inside all of us. "Like scrambled eggs. Messy, soft, and okay, I'm okay, I can do this," she said while looking at me with a big smile.

The "felt sense" was coined by Gene Gendlin when he and Carl Rogers set out to understand why some people are stuck in therapy and others change. By observing people and studying what happens in sessions, they saw that positive and lasting change happened when people could access the nonverbal, body-feel of the issues that were challenging them. Realizing that people can learn this skill, Gendlin created a six-step method for discovering and using the felt sense for personal development. Having trained in this process, I developed Power-Pausing to access our felt sense in our daily lives at work, at home, and on the go.

When listening inside with an attitude of curiosity and intention to understand how we feel and what we need, we can create meaning and a new connection with our emotional well-being. We do this by using temperature, color, images, metaphors, or energetically relating to how it feels in there, like "jittery" or "bubbly" for example. It might not make sense to others, but it has meaning to each of us and gives us a way to relate and communicate with ourselves about how we feel inside. It's a powerful tool for using our self-awareness to harness change and reclaim agency over our emotional well-being, unlocking the connection between our body-awareness and our emotional-awareness.

Self-awareness is a big topic among leaders who recognize the need for new skills to communicate with empathy, engage better with their people, and create a respectful workplace. We all need emotional well-being to harness our mental health and cultivate work-life quality. It's easy to ignore and dismiss how we feel inside when we are busy and want to get stuff done; however, it's a misunderstanding of what self-awareness can do for us. I think of emotions as the doorway to a better connection with ourselves and each other, as information that helps us make better decisions, and as an intuitive connection that helps us harness creativity and innovation.

PAUSE ON THIS

We can only foster a healthy relationship with others to the extent that we have one with ourselves.

- If we are constantly being critical of ourselves, how can we be curious about others?

  _____

  _____

- If we ignore our emotions, how can we engage empathetically with others?

  _____

  _____

- If we feel like we don't matter, how can we show up in a way that makes us feel included?

  _____

  _____

- If we feel we are not worthy of care and attention, how can we expect to get our needs met?

  _____

  _____

Emotions Are Good

We need emotions. It's part of how we navigate any relationship and make better decisions. Thinking that we don't have emotions at work is a misunderstanding of how emotions work. We talk about the Great Resignation as people leaving their jobs; however, feeling resigned is also a lack of motivation. To be motivated, we need emotions. In effect, we lose our motivation when our heart is no longer in it. We might think we do things for money and status, but we essentially do things because of what we care about. When we no longer care, we lose motivation. Isn't that so?

Emotions are what make us human. Suppressing emotions is unfair to our emotional intelligence and hiding how we feel instead of having a conversation that could further the understanding and bridge the divide keeps us stuck in emotional insecurity. So, on one hand, we think of emotions as disruption and on the other hand, we want to feel something to feel alive. Can you see the contradiction?

What I see changing at work is the need for and the power of emotional integration at work and the impact that has on our mental health. Not only does it make us happier when we are inclusive of our emotional selves but using our emotions as information is also how we increase innovation, productivity, and effective communication. And it's essential to creating a healthy culture.

Emotions at Work

Emotions are tied to how we think and what we do, and as whole humans, we integrate our emotions so that we can think, engage, and act with more care and purpose. I know you might be thinking emotions cloud our judgment, and to perform our best, we have to leave our emotions behind when we start the workday. But what if that's all wrong?

Let's make something a little clearer about the difference between having emotions and being emotional. Being emotional is a behavior that comes from suppressing, ignoring, and hiding from our emotions and eventually they come out, often in anger or distress. We reach a boiling-over point where we simply cannot hold it in any longer. By learning the tools to listen better, we can understand our emotions and use them to communicate how we feel and what we need so that we can be more constructive, creative, and collaborative, which essentially is how we access our emotional intelligence.

Emotional intelligence is an essential factor in our work environment today and in the future. However, it can easily be misunderstood as managing emotions, getting them under control, taming them, and even "man-handling" them. Sure, sometimes we need to get back to our emotions later or suspend worry until we know more, but that's different from ignoring them and telling them that they are not welcome as emotions are essential to our well-being.

Back when I was a gymnast, we had to suspend worry and other emotions until we were done with the training, or we would not be in the right mindset to focus. We often need to do that at work; however, to do so, we first must acknowledge how we feel because if not, our emotions are like a puppy, constantly wanting our attention. We can push them aside and try to ignore them, but that doesn't work. Instead, if we tell our emotions we'll get back to them after this next meeting, it's like giving the puppy a bone to chew on for the next hour, and we can reclaim our focus. That's the power of the mind and emotional integration.

Emotions as Information

You might have heard people say that emotions are *energy moving through*. This is not meant to dismiss that we can be in emotional distress and emotions such as grief and sadness, fear and anxiety don't feel like a transient emotional wave of energy for those who struggle with living in these states most of the time. Having grown up with a bipolar mother and having worked with mental health for many years, it's unfair to anyone living with depression to make emotional health about waves of energy passing through. But there's also a truth to this that we cannot deny. Emotions are tied to our hormones and nervous system, which we know fluctuate throughout the day, especially when working under chronic stress.

When I studied mind-body-social health, I discovered that survival stress—the fear that something may hurt you, causing your body to naturally respond with a burst of energy so you can survive the dangerous situation (fight) or escape it altogether (flight)—was one of three categories: sad, mad, or scared. These core emotions go back to our instinctive reactions to defend ourselves from danger, secure belonging by avoiding separation and exclusion from the community, and loss of territory, which at work we would call "power" or "position."

This is why Power-Pausing is a crucial change that allows us a moment in time to be curious about what we need to better navigate our changing day-to-day emotions, which are constantly affected by our environment.

We are constantly feeling our way through our world. Someone says something and we feel something. We hear a tune on the radio and we feel something. We hear about someone who just did an amazing job and we feel something. We hear someone just lost someone and we feel something. We read something and we feel something. We think about something that has happened in the past and we feel something. We are constantly in an emotional relationship with ourselves and the world around us. We cannot ignore or isolate ourselves from it, or else, it will make us emotional.

The FUD (fear, uncertainty, and doubt) is uncomfortable, messy, and even chaotic at times. However, it's also information that's helped us survive and inform us about danger. We talked about navigating FUD earlier and recognizing stress as the pothole that we steer clear of. However, we can pause for a moment and ask what we need so that we can become comfortable with the discomfort. Change creates tension. It doesn't mean something is wrong; it's just how change affects us. But we are conditioned to avoid tension and instead of using it to create change and more flow in our lives, resisting listening to the tension is actually how we get stuck in non-action.

In mindfulness practice, we use emotions as information by observing them rather than fixing them. We can befriend our emotions and get to know them better. This way they no longer control our lives because we no longer rush to react and fix how we feel, but rather, we stay with the discomfort for just a little longer to let it inform us in our choices and decisions. This is how we use Power-Pausing to listen and ask how we are feeling in there and ask what we need so that we can better respond with care.

Similarly, in hypnotherapy, we look for our own inner resources to navigate *what is*. We cannot change what happened but we can change our relationship with what's possible now. We cannot control the future but we can ask what we need so that we can feel capable and ready to navigate what might come. That's how FUD can be used as information: recognizing the emotion and asking what we need to be more comfortable with the discomfort. I think of it as a way to open up to ourselves and our lives in an empathetic, curious, and care-driven manner.

Emotional Respect

I want to be clear that I'm not speaking as a psychotherapist but as a mental health coach. In no way am I saying that we can solve emotional distress by asking better questions. It's important that you reach out for help when going through difficult times and need to talk about it. If you struggle with depression and anxiety, ask for help! Please don't think you need to fix yourself and go at it alone. More and more companies are offering mental health programs and access to getting support. Use the tools you have, all of them. Talking to a mental health professional is important both for our private and professional well-being because as whole humans, it's all interconnected.

There's a fine line between being a whole human at work and also recognizing our emotional responsibility to discuss something in private versus at work. I often hear people wonder about what to share and when we are oversharing. For example, you might not want to hear about your manager's dating life, but you do want to know if your manager is going through a divorce or death in the family because you want to be supportive of the stress that adds to anyone's life. Just like you can tell when someone is happy and enjoying feeling loved, you can tell when someone is sad. Emotions, like stress, are contagious as are joy, happiness, and well-being. The point is, we don't have to be one thing or the other; the point is to communicate what we are going through so those around us don't have to guess.

When listening to our emotions and being self-aware, we can start to learn how to recognize what we need. When we worry about something, we can wonder what we need to feel more secure, not by rejecting our worry but by listening to the worry and recognizing that our self-awareness can be used to know more about ourselves.

Emotional Agency

When people say we cannot have emotions at work, we need to understand what they are referring to. Yelling at someone is not an emotion; it's a behavior that comes from suppressing our FUD until we cannot hold it any longer. Listening to our emotions and communicating what's going on AND asking ourselves what we need so that we can feel okay right now is being transparent and authentic. That is how we reclaim emotional agency because we cannot hide from our emotions.

By embracing Power-Pausing, we can observe our emotions and allow them to inform our behavior, which may be to do nothing and simply let our emotions be our emotions.

The point is to learn to pause before we react so we choose how to respond and act, whether that's communicating to others that something is going on that's worrying us, communicating when we are excited and happy about something, or just taking a moment to ourselves.

Often people guess what others feel instead of us having the language and tools to communicate it. Empathetic people think of their self-awareness as a way to understand others, and it can be; however, we can also pause, listen, and ask more questions to cultivate empathetic conversations.

Self-Awareness Is Also Self-Acceptance

Acknowledging how we feel and choosing to shift the focus to be curious about what we need to feel better is how we can use our emotions in a more immediate way to inform us in connecting, communicating, and collaborating better.

Remember how the mind will answer what you ask it, and you can use the awareness to shift your focus onto feeling confident. Start practicing in small ways by asking yourself these questions as you go through your day, pause, listen inside, and ask, "Hey how am I in there right now? What do I need so that I can. . .?" These questions help you focus on how you want to feel instead of the feelings you are trying to avoid.

I think of my emotions as a way to give me a poke about what I need to pay attention to. If I'm nervous about something, I pause on that and ask myself more questions about it. Then I use that to inform my decisions, which may be that I need even more information.

When in conversation with others, I can use my emotional self-awareness to navigate my interaction and conversation by being more conscious about how I feel and with that, how that shows up in my dialog. We might feel nervous about something and we try to avoid or ignore certain aspects and control the conversation to steer away from what we are nervous about while knowing all along that we are not being completely authentic. Instead, we can use our concerns as information to wonder what we need to be able to address certain topics. This is how we use self-awareness to connect, communicate, and collaborate better.

Recently I spoke with a leader who was concerned about addressing a mass shooting with her team and she thought it would be best to leave it be and avoid discussing it, not sure how different people felt about gun control. We discussed how she didn't have to control the conversation but rather facilitate pauses to hold space for people to speak if they wanted to express how they felt. She contacted me the day after and expressed relief that she had started the meeting asking if they wanted to talk about it as it had turned into a vulnerable, honest, and bonding team meeting.

Sometimes we know we are nervous about a conversation, and we can prepare ourselves to feel more ready. Other times though, we are triggered and we need to adjust on the go, especially when we don't know what we are walking into. It's important we allow our emotions to inform us by pausing so we can hold space for ourselves and each other rather than reacting to defend and protect how we feel. This is also how we can pause together, listen to each other, ask more questions, and align with common values that we can agree on.

That's also why pausing before we answer is essential to not end up regretting our reactions. A past client told me how he had been stressed at work and after arriving home had snapped at his wife, only to spend the entire evening in a fight over his behavior. This for sure is not a great way to unstress after work. After talking it out with me, he agreed that he could have returned home, communicated how concerned he was feeling about work, and asked his wife to listen to him talk through it.

Let's use the pause to come back home to ourselves, back to feeling grounded in ourselves, and then choosing how to best respond so that we can reclaim emotional agency.

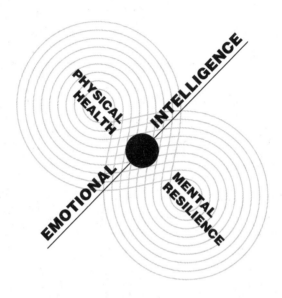

It's best to start out practicing this in situations that are low-stress so that we are not expected to harness our self-awareness when under pressure and in high-stress situations. Use daily situations where you can pause before action, just to start learning to use your attention to create more awareness of your patterns.

PAUSE ON THIS

Mindfulness practice is about observing our thoughts without running after them. Emotional awareness is the same practice; observing and acknowledging how we feel without having to fix anything because having emotions is what makes us human.

- Try to note some of the emotions you feel on an average day and see if you can "let them be" and allow them to talk to you.

  _____

  _____

- Notice if you have the impulse to fix or get rid of how you feel, and what it might feel like if you simply said, "That's okay, thank you for letting me know," to the emotions as they come up.

  _____

  _____

We need to embrace that it's okay to feel as it's a big part of our emotional and mental well-being. Learning to listen, truly listen, is how we start to learn about ourselves and each other and the key to reclaiming agency over our lives.

CHAPTER 12

Self-Responsibility

"What do I need so that I can. . .?"

"I'm concerned that I'm burning out before reaching the top of my career. I'm always exhausted because I don't sleep because of my kids. I'm 35 years old, and I feel like I can't last much longer."

This was the concern of a young man I met during a training for rising young leaders. But instead of jumping straight into giving him suggestions about how to get better or more sleep, I paused and asked, "Tell me more; your kids are young. Are they not sleeping well?"

"No, that's not it," he replied. "They're not that young, they're eight and nine years old, and they sleep fine." I was confused and asked him to tell me more. "After they go to bed, I have to watch sports, and then it gets late, and I have to get up again at 5 a.m. I simply don't get enough sleep."

In unison, people around him began nodding in agreement as it seemed like they could relate to the problem of going to bed too late because of their kids.

"Okay, so let me get this right," I replied. "You don't get enough sleep because you stay up late watching sports? It's not because of your kids; it's because you want to watch sports after they go to bed? I completely understand that you want some down-time to end your day without commitments and responsibilities. However, the story you are telling yourself is that you are exhausted and burning out because of your kids. Can you see that staying up late is your choice?"

He agreed and slowly nodded. I could tell he was processing what he had just experienced. He felt seen and heard for wanting some self-time at night, and he also realized that he was blaming his kids for his lack of sleep, and therefore, not taking responsibility for his self-care.

When we blame others for our choices, we give away our power to have agency over our lives and our self-care. As a result, we can end up becoming resentful and staying stuck instead of building a support system inclusive of our commitments and responsibilities to work, others, and ourselves and our need to have moments of not having to care about anything.

"Yes, But. . ."

We "Yes, but. . ." ourselves all the time. It's part of the inner dialog and the paradoxes we explored earlier in this book. We get used to our daily habits and routines as they become automatic and mindless. Some of our behaviors are inherited from our family and have followed us since childhood, and others are adapted to fit in and belong. There is nothing right or wrong about this; the question is whether or not these behaviors are working for us.

To take responsibility for our choices, actions, and habits we must first be honest with ourselves. In fact, the most powerful, yet the most difficult decision we can make is to be bluntly honest with ourselves.

Are we choosing to avoid pain and pursue immediate relief through pleasure? Or are we willing to go through the discomfort of leaving something we enjoy behind to achieve what it takes to feel better overall?

The reality is that most people choose immediate pleasure. We want instant gratification and relief from whatever pain, frustration, emotion, and stressors we want to avoid feeling and facing. It's just human behavior. There's nothing wrong with you. However, taking responsibility is essential to harnessing change and growth, and sometimes we must let go of what we have to get what we want.

When I first started working with hypnotherapy, I didn't do so to fix bad habits and give people new ones by the time they woke up from the trance. I wanted to understand where our human motivation comes from, and I wanted to learn how we could get unstuck from the stories we tell ourselves that hold us back from harnessing change and growth.

Self-doubt gets in the way of change. We listen to what other people think we should do and what they think we are capable of doing. The key to change is to recognize our own patterns and see where we can shift our choices.

We "should" ourselves so much, and it's not working for us because when we "should" ourselves we give the power of decision over to someone else, and we also shame ourselves.

I consistently saw that even though my clients wanted to change their habits, they first had to change their thinking. A big part of this is rooted in two major belief systems: that we cannot handle discomfort and therefore seek relief from pain with pleasure, and thinking we have to always please and take care of others before we take care of ourselves.

At work, it can mean overstepping boundaries. Your manager doesn't take lunch and you feel you need to skip it too. Your manager sends emails after work hours and you think you have to respond then. Meetings are added to your schedule even when you had the time blocked out and you feel that you have to show up. Now you probably will say, "Yes, but. . ." because when it's about work, we are trained to believe we have to say yes. But if you feel you have to say yes every time, you might end up blaming others for not being able to reclaim self-care in your day and feel even more powerless for it.

I want to pause here and make one thing clear—this is not about blaming you for letting your boundaries slide. Most people don't even recognize this is happening because we are socially trained to think that we have to please others, fit in, and belong whether it's for our team or our family. We do not learn that being inclusive of our own needs means we can be there better and stronger for others and for our work. It's not part of our social construct. Yet, self-care is about recognizing that the more we accept and embrace our own needs, the more we can be in full expression, give our best self, and thereby feel that we belong.

Creating a respectful work culture starts with respecting ourselves and our needs, and that starts with taking responsibility for them too. I am not saying it's only up to each of us to create the change because we need the culture to change as well. A healthy work environment is one that acknowledges that we work better when self-care is the foundation for how we reach our goals. Instead of our current culture that has us feeling like we need permission to pause and using language like "giving ourselves permission" to take a moment to reset, refocus, and reclaim our energy, we must build a culture where cultivating work-life quality is the norm. Where we all take a moment to think before we engage and act. What if we had a culture where we needed permission *not* to pause? A culture where we cultivated a mutual effort to respect each other for having needs?

It's a complete change in how we think. Like a lot of people, you probably grew up with the message that it's selfish to think of yourself first. The thing is, taking care of yourself and getting your needs met is not selfish at all; it's actually more selfish not to because you are not at your best. You might not even be as nice when you are tired, exhausted, irritable, and feeling like you don't matter.

To cultivate a healthier working environment, we must learn to be more inclusive of our needs so that we don't abandon ourselves to please others. Instead of thinking that our needs are unwelcome, habits are a chore and a challenge, and change is an impossibility that adds to feeling overwhelmed, how do we pause to listen better to ourselves? How do we reclaim a moment to cut through the overwhelm? How do we learn to understand why what we need really matters? How do we take back agency to build a self-supportive environment? How can we be open and flexible with what other people need from us and also hold self-respecting, self-caring boundaries so each of us has what we need to succeed?

Without changing our minds about that, we stay stuck thinking that tomorrow we will do better, but today we need to abandon ourselves for just another day. We do this because we care about other people, our work, and we care about how we show up. I'm asking you to completely change the way you think of taking responsibility for what your day looks like and how you achieve the results you want to achieve. It's not about saying no to others. It's about saying "Yes, and" to yourself and them.

We can only navigate a constantly changing reality and harness growth when well-being is the foundation for how we work and live better, together.

PAUSE ON THIS

- What are typical situations where you "Yes, but. . ." yourself and do what someone else wants because you have to choose between what they want and what you need?

_____

_____

- What boundaries do you typically uphold, and which do you ignore and overstep?

_____

_____

- What do you care about and put first so that it gets in the way of respecting your needs and boundaries?

_____

_____

- When you choose to hold a strong, healthy, and caring boundary for yourself, how does it feel and why does it matter?

_____

_____

"Yes, And. . ."

"When we say yes to others, we say no to ourselves." There's a lot of truth to this popular phrase. However, there's a flip side to this, one that takes pause and honesty to recognize—when we say yes to others, we also say yes to something we need.

For example, you might say yes to taking on another project task—you want to be seen as someone capable, and you are looking to grow, even if you're already fully committed and know it's going to cost you your free time. Or you might say yes to a meeting you don't have time for because you hope you will learn something useful or have an opportunity to contribute in a way that makes you feel more valuable. Or you might say yes to helping a friend because you are afraid to upset them, even though you want some time off.

Think about the previous sentences and recognize your pattern. We all do it; the point is to be honest about it as that's how we reclaim agency because at the end of the day, it's the choices we make that make our day.

The "Yes, and" inclusive way of looking at getting your needs met means taking a pause to ask yourself: "How am I in there right now, and what do I need so that I can. . . whatever it is you need to do right now?"

Habit-Shifting

"Yes, but I don't have time to change my habits." I've heard this many times, and I constantly challenge people by asking them why it takes more time to buy a healthy snack than an unhealthy one? The reality is that it doesn't take more time; it takes more effort, which means we have to pay attention and be willing to go through the uncomfortable stage of change. We don't like changing habits, even when that's what we want.

Habits are a collection of choices, and 95 percent of them are unconscious and automatic. Some of them are ones we don't pay attention to and make up our daily routine, like getting out of bed, taking a shower, and brushing your teeth. Some are the ones that get us stuck that we don't take responsibility for (like surfing the Internet when what we really need is to Power-Pausing). The remaining 5 percent, the ones we pay attention to, are the ones that create changes and culminate into the person you want to be. The more we Power-Pausing, the more we can tap into that 5 percent to help us use our unconscious habits more intentionally.

We can look at breaking down habits into three buckets:

- **Automatic habits:** These are reaction-based and are mostly mindless and unconscious. Even though these habits get us through the day, some of them may not be serving us any-more, especially not at work, where reactions tend to flare up when we are under stress.

- **Craving habits:** These make us do things "for just one more day" even if we promised ourselves we would stop because the pain of not getting the instant gratification is just too uncom-fortable. We humans make choices based on fear or desire, what we want to avoid or what we care about. Under stress, it's what we want to avoid—the discomfort of anxiety—that takes over. I also like to call these "avoidance habits" as they are the ones we wish we could change but feel powerless over.

- **Change habits:** These we choose to put our attention toward in order to create change. Remember, intention fuels attention. So we commit and work on the steps that create the change we want by building in small micro-changes instead of big leaps; I call it habit shifting. The small stuff adds up and leads us in a new direction, which leads to dif-ferent outcomes and a new way of going through the day. These habits take intention and attention, which means we need to pause and be mindful.

We Don't Have to Fit into Our Habits; Our Habits Have to Fit Us

No matter how tempting, and no matter how much something may work for someone else, we don't have to fit into the same habits as other people. Self-care means different things to different people; it will not even be the same for you throughout the month, week, or even day.

We need different things at different times, mainly because our habits are supposed to support us in getting through our challenges. This is where we end up abandoning our self-care when work and life get busy because we have an ideal of what self-care is supposed to look like, and we end up should-ing ourselves only to end up feeling worse. I hear this all the time and it compounds the challenge we have integrating work and life.

The mindset that self-care is either/or is not a helpful one. I know many coaches talk about commitment, to just do it, and you must stick to it. However, this message only works for some people. Schedule what you would like to do so you can set up your day, but please don't think that there's only one way to self-care.

To own our habits is how we can be our most powerful. To choose our actions based on what we want to achieve and what we need to succeed in any given moment is how we can become more adaptable and agile. And the way we self-care plays a starring role in this as it's how we truly support ourselves in working better.

When we change our relationship with our habits and think of them as choices that we make to support ourselves as a whole human we are using The Self-Care Mindset®. This allows us to harness our self-care by being more aware—pausing for a moment to listen, ask, and then choose what we need right now so that we can align with what we are doing. Yes, make plans for how you achieve your goals and what you need to accomplish them.

However, please know that the small things you do to support yourself all day are the very things that help you win the day.

How to Make Your Habits Work for You

Getting to know what you need is the first step to making your habits fit you instead of getting stuck, constantly feeling like you are not doing enough, and allowing your self-talk and inner critic to continually point out what's not working. Your inner critic might say, "I'll never get this to work," whereas your inner coach would say, "What do I need so that I can make this work?" Remember, changing the question changes your focus and therefore, changes the outcome.

Foundational Self-Care Habits

Let's not get fancy about self-care. Let's start with the basics before we add all the gym memberships, monthly massages, and weekly manicures. Self-care should not cost money or take time away from us. It's supposed to support us in working better and spending time more effectively.

YOUR WHOLE HEALTH
IS YOUR OPERATING SYSTEM

WATER
1/2 YOUR BODY WEIGHT IN OUNCES
STAYING HYDRATED KEEPS YOUR MIND ALERT,
FOCUS ENGAGED, ENERGY VIBRANT, AND YOUR MOOD AGILE

FOOD
3 MEALS A DAY, KEEPS YOUR GLUCOSE LEVELS STEADY
12 HOURS FASTING OVERNIGHT, ALLOWS RECOVERY
4 HOURS BETWEEN MEALS, MANAGES YOUR ENERGY

REST & RESET
SLEEP 7 1/2 HOURS (NOT JUST IN BED)
PAUSES EVERY 45-90 MINUTES TO RESET, RECOVER, REFOCUS
TAKE LUNCH—MAKE SPACE BETWEEN MEETINGS

The most basic self-care essentials are a basic human right: water, food, and sleep. When I ask people if they drink enough water, eat their meals, and practice good sleep hygiene every day, most say no to at least one of them, even though we live in a modern world where these three things are accessible. Poverty has risen since COVID. However, these essentials must still be regarded as essentials.

I had a boss many years ago in the fashion industry who told me he didn't eat lunch, so he didn't see why I needed to either. I'm not sure where I got the guts, but I looked at him and said, "I need to eat."

Getting permission to drink water, eat food, go for bathroom breaks, take small breaks to recover, and stop working late so we can get our sleep should not be a discussion we need to have at this point in our human evolution. To succeed in the future of work, we must respect and reclaim our most basic human needs. Without it, we keep the toxic survival hustle culture alive, where we are not appreciated for who we are. The discussion I have most with leaders and executives these days is around the question of, "How do we take better care of our people?" My answer is to always start by giving them the basic tools of self-care to make a culture change. Let's normalize self-care at work, even the most basic form; that's just human and by the way, it's smart too. The organ that uses the most energy all day long is our brain. We need to feed it a proper meal to work smarter.

WATER • FOOD • PAUSE • REST
SELF-CARE WORK HABITS TO SUPPORT YOUR NATURAL RHYTHM

MORNING	MID-MORNING	LUNCH	AFTERNOON	EVENING
BREAKFAST TO GET ACTIVATED	PAUSE AND CHECK IN	PAUSE AND REFUEL	PAUSE AND CHECK IN	DINNER TO SETTLE DOWN
MORNING ROUTINES TO START AND PREPARE FOR THE DAY AHEAD.	WHEN DO YOU WORK OPTIMALLY AND WHAT DO YOU NEED TO DO YOUR BEST WORK?	WHAT HAVE YOU ACHIEVED SO FAR AND WHAT DO YOU NEED TO OPTIMIZE THE REST OF THE DAY?	WHAT DO YOU NEED FOR THE AFTERNOON TO BE PRODUCTIVE?	LET BE AND LET GO. RETIRE, RETREAT, RECOVER. CREATE SPACE BETWEEN ACTION AND NON-ACTION.

MINDFUL MOMENT MEDITATION	WATER / TEA / COFFEE	WATER / TEA	WATER / TEA	MINDFUL MOMENT MEDITATION
BRAIN-DUMP / JOURNALING	PEE BREAK	FOOD TO RELAX AND RETHINK	PEE BREAK	BRAIN-DUMP / JOURNALING
FOCUSING MOMENT (AAA)	WALK OR JUMPING JACKS	FOOD TO RE-ENERGIZE AND RESET?	WALK OR JUMPING JACKS	FOCUSING MOMENT (AAA)
STRETCH	STRETCH	FEED YOUR PHYSICAL, EMOTIONAL, AND MENTAL BODY	STRETCH	STRETCH
MOVEMENT	PAUSE		PAUSE	MOVEMENT
FAMILY	BREATHE WITH INTENT		BREATHE WITH INTENT	FAMILY
FOOD	CHECK IN WITH SOMEONE		CHECK IN WITH SOMEONE	FOOD
WATER	LOOK OUTSIDE		LOOK OUTSIDE	WATER
PETS	SHIFT YOUR BRAIN OFF FOR 5		SHIFT YOUR BRAIN OFF FOR 5	PETS
PREPARE FOR THE DAY				LET GO OF THE DAY

Look at your schedule and put in a lunch break. Just like when we were in school, lunch breaks go on the schedule, and so do pauses to get ready for the next meeting. Without putting it on the schedule, we will not respect the time for it because as the day progresses, we will schedule over it, forgetting that we need food to ensure our brain works optimally. You can always move it, but please don't cancel your health. A leader I worked with always called it a "meeting with himself." We need to respect those meetings as much as the meeting we have with our team and managers. I know, you might be looking at your schedule right now and thinking, "Where in the world am I going to put this?" The answer: Plan ahead, have a conversation with your team and your manager and discuss how to fit in human pauses to nourish your body and mind as it helps both you, your work, and everyone's shared stress levels to stay healthy.

Companies are beginning to increasingly recognize that business is no longer work as usual and that a thriving culture is based on human connection. But we can only access what makes us human if we treat ourselves humanely. The future of work isn't slowing down, so it's up to us to do it ourselves and this starts with a lunch break, where we don't work while eating. If you are already doing that, add in some 5–15 minute Power-Pausing between meetings roughly every 45–90 minutes to get you physically, emotionally, and mentally ready for the next meeting.

The bottom line is we don't get time or find time; we make time and take time.

Using self-awareness, we can start noticing our strengths and where we need more support throughout the day. Again, this is not a stagnant picture. You might recognize that your energy, focus, and attention change throughout the day. We start finding stability in our day by learning to balance through change. I'm a firm believer that we have balance all wrong. We think it's about peacefulness and quiet, where we are not troubled and worried. I think of balance as continuously navigating what comes our way without losing focus and attention on what matters.

There's an old story about a student who asks his Kung Fu master if he will ever be able to keep his balance as well as the master to which the master answers, "I don't have more balance than you; I just find it faster when I lose it."

Similarly, you can watch a ballerina. They may look like they have perfect balance and are perfectly still and graceful from a distance. When you get close though, you see that their legs and feet are constantly at work with tiny movements to keep their balance. In the same way, we need to stop thinking that balance is something we find and then keep. Instead, it's how we keep asking what we need so that we can cope and deal with what comes our way to navigate change and harness growth with these constant adjustments, or we can end up feeling kicked off course by change.

Let's stop wasting time discussing what's not working and instead keep asking what we each need to make work work better for us.

Plot Out Your Day

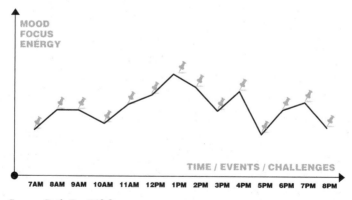

Source: Path For Life®

You might want to do this for a few days to see how the week progresses.

- Draw a line from left to right, putting in the hours of the day from the time you get up till the time you go to bed.

- From the bottom left-side to top left-side, draw another line upward from 1 to 10 that has energy, focus, mood, creativity, and attention.

- Plot in your highs and lows while noticing how you feel as the day goes on within that range of what you want to track.

- If you want to use different colors, you can. You will find that energy, focus, attention, and mood will oftentimes follow each other. Creativity, focus, and mood will have similarities too, as we have different kinds of focus and moods for different things.

- Note your stress and emotional agility as well. Does it wear out as the day goes on? Or do you find that it changes based on what happens and how you support yourself in navigating challenges?

- The key is to notice the changes more than getting the number right. It's a great way to start asking and recognizing that we need different things to support feeling optimally throughout the day instead of just pushing through the slumps.

Along the same lines, start from the left and start plotting how you feel first thing in the morning to gauge your energy, focus, mood, stress levels, and to determine if you feel anxious or excited. As the day progresses, you can continue by gaining clarity on when you feel most creative and focused as well as when you feel more productive working alone and working with your team.

We all have different peak times throughout the day. When you start noticing how your energy, focus, and attention changes throughout the day by plotting it out, you can identify your peak times to gain clarity on when you focus best on your own work and when the best times are for meetings with others. Of equal importance, by plotting out your day, you can also learn when you most need recovery time too.

What Do You Need So That You Can. . .?

Start to use the previous chart and then ask yourself what you need when you feel like. . .whatever it is you are feeling in the moment. Remember to ask questions in a way that allows you to focus on how you want to feel so that you can leverage your curiosity and both your conscious and unconscious mind to find the answers.

Here are some examples of how to ask the questions and what you might need when you feel tired and what to do to get more energy:

- **Water:** feeling tired, sleepy, confused, hangry, irritable, and even angry are the first signs of dehydration. You might want to think about water pauses throughout the day.

- **Food:** avoid sugar and opt for more of a "real meal" or protein/plant-fat-rich snack. Think of something that is a lean protein with some veggies and choose complex carbs over high-starch carbs like bread and pasta, which might just make you drowsy.

- **Coffee:** opt for tea instead and water first to avoid the spike and crash. Needing energy might simply be dehydration, not a need for a stimulant like coffee.

- **Retreat to recover:** have you been focusing on the same thing for too long? If so, disconnect to reconnect.

- **Nap:** studies show a 10-minute nap gives you more energy than coffee and is more sustainable and long-lasting.

- **Stretch:** get up from your chair and stretch your lower back by leaning over forward or standing up and swinging and twisting. You can also lean over your legs with your arms to the floor while letting your head hang down.

- **Walk:** my favorite reason to take a couple of 15-minute breaks is that my dog and I need to get out and get some fresh air throughout the day. I tend to do a quick walk to get the blood pumping and my energy circulation going again.

- **Do jumping jacks or dance:** just a simple way to get your body moving. Plus, both activities are fun as it's hard to feel worse after dancing or doing jumping jacks.

- **Sing:** we can get tired because we aren't using our breath well, and when we sing, we start breathing more.

- **Take some nice big inhales:** when we want more energy, the inhale is what we need to focus on as opposed to the exhale, which helps us calm down. You can inhale for 7 counts and then simply let go of the breath as it's a nice way to build up some energy.

- **Energy tapping:** tap lightly on the top of your head with your fingertips about 10 times, then the top of your eyebrows, then top of your upper lip, just under the collar bone on each side where it meets where there's like a little soft spot, and then along the side of the body aligned with your breasts/chest, and to end, tap the side of the hands. Do this round three times. It's called EFT, Emotional Freedom Technic. Even the army uses it to manage stress.

- **Shoulder and neck massage stretches:** roll your shoulders a bit and wiggle your upper body and lean your head from side to side, forward, and back.

Keep going and make your own energy go-to list.

Following the same thread, when you feel distracted, ask yourself, "What do I need to reclaim my attention and focus?" Again, make your own list.

- **Get up and move:** Maybe you have been sitting too long while working on the same thing. We might not notice it but we can get lost in mind-wandering if we are stuck in a problem. Instead of stepping away to reclaim our attention, we end up trying to solve the wrong problem while our mind is somewhere else.

- **Get rid of distraction:** We all know how those notifications can get to us. Consider reserving 45–90 minutes for deep work where your phone is out of sight and all email or notifications are silenced so you can better focus on what's in front of you.

- **Make a note to pause before you react:** I often hear people regret they said something or yelled at someone, and it became a distraction until they apologized. This is one of the reasons why pausing can save you time. Pause before you react means you don't have to fix something later, wasting time being distracted thinking about what you regret.

- **Put your worries down on paper:** We can be rather distracted when there's something we have left undone. Deciding when we are going to do it and getting it down on paper is one way to let it be until then.

- **Ask for clarification on pending items:** Waiting is a distraction for sure. Sometimes you can ask when to expect it so that you don't waste time thinking about it. Other times you simply have to make a choice to put something aside until you get the answer. Making a conscious choice tends to help our minds stop thinking about it.

As a reminder, you can check the previous list when you are tired and need more energy too because having energy and reclaiming attention and focus sometimes need the same thing.

When You Feel the FUD

FUD is a major distraction and the way to navigate it begins by asking yourself, "What do I need so that I can reclaim agency and steer past the FUD?" To see this in action, let's explore these following questions.

FEAR: What do I need so that I can feel safe, able to manage, and confident that I'm capable?

UNCERTAINTY: What do I need so that I can have more clarity, courage, and confidence?

DOUBT: What do I need so that I can feel more certain and safer?

Maybe you need to think through a plan in case the worst-case scenario happens so you realize you can trust yourself to figure it out. Maybe you need to ask what you need to get the confidence that you can handle it. For example, say you are scared that you are going to get laid off. In this case, ask yourself:

- What do I need so that I can feel safe that I will find a new job?

- What do I need so that I can feel safe that I am not on the list?

- What do I need to have more confidence that I'm a desirable candidate for another position?

- And last, ask yourself, "What do I need to suspend worry until I know more?"

To quote the Dalai Lama: "If there is no solution to the problem then don't waste time worrying about it. If there is a solution to the problem then don't waste time worrying about it." Easier said than done, I know. But regardless, it's powerful.

Be specific when you ask the questions so that you can trigger your inner resources to find more questions that lead to some of the answers you are looking for. FUD is a mixture of emotions, so don't spend time deciding which emotion it is as the reality is that we have many different emotions, even at the same time. FUD is a bit of a "bundle of emotions" itself. The rest of this chapter looks at examples of what to tell your mind you are looking for and what you want to feel like.

Working with the FUD

Take some of the emotions you feel on a daily basis from Chapter 11, "Self-Awareness." Write them down, then next to them, write what you would like to feel instead. You can even use fear, anxiety, and confusion that comes from FUD as a framework for the questions you ask yourself.

How am I in there? I feel scared:

- What do I need so that I can feel safe?

- What do I need so that I can trust more and feel secure?

- What do I need so that I can be hopeful and joyful?

How am I in there? I feel uncertain:

- What do I need so that I can have more clarity?

- What do I need so that I can feel more courageous?

- What do I need so that I can feel more certain and grounded?

How am I in there? I feel anxious:

- What do I need so that I can have more confidence?

- What do I need so that I can feel more in control?

- What do I need so that I can feel safe?

How am I in there? I feel overwhelmed:

- What do I need so that I can cut through the noise and organize my thoughts?

- What do I need so that I can have more clarity and feel more in control?

- What do I need so that I can feel more empowered and confident?

How am I in there? I feel sad:

- What do I need so that I can feel more curious?

- What do I need so that I can have more excited?

- What do I need so that I can feel more joyful?

How am I in there? I feel alone:

- What do I need so that I can feel more included?

- What do I need so that I can feel more connected?

- What do I need so that I can feel I belong?

Keep asking yourself how you are in there throughout the day. Sometimes just noticing is enough to feel better. Like Socrates said, *"Care for your psyche—know thyself, for once we know ourselves, we may learn how to care for ourselves."*

Motivation for Change

An Olympic swimmer was asked about how he found the motivation to get up every morning at 3 a.m. to train before going to work, and his answer was not surprising. He shared how he did not want to get up and go swimming at that hour, but he absolutely did want the gold medal. He also shared that once he was in the water, he knew that's exactly where he needed to be. We might not be motivated by the prospect of doing something, like working out. It's the goal we are trying to achieve that motivates us to take responsibility for our choices, actions, and habits. However, this is only the case if it's something we genuinely care about, and we must enjoy the process of achieving it.

We can get hard on ourselves when we don't feel motivated, can't we? That inner critic has a field day when we are procrastinating and don't feel like doing what we had all the best intentions of doing.

When clients came to get coached, wanting to get healthy, I would ask them, "Why now?" They would then reply by saying things like, "I know it's time!" "I should pay more attention to my health!" "I want to feel better and lose weight so I can fit into my clothes!" These may seem like excellent reasons, but they're not. We need to take it a step further and ask ourselves why it matters that we get healthy. How it will impact us and our lives beyond being healthy? Zeroing in on what it's for and who it's for and why it matters in the greater sense is where we connect with the true purpose of our choices.

One client, who was in her later years, told me how she's struggled with change and motivation to get healthy for the past 35 years. "It never works. Nothing works," she said. But when we paused for a bit longer on the questions of "What's it for? And why does that matter?" we got closer to what she cared about, and she was able to take responsibility for the new habits that she wanted to learn. It turns out, she wanted to be able to keep up with her grandchild, and she wanted to be around for him. That's what she deeply cared about. It wasn't about her and her health itself, but rather what her health could do for her.

For us to change our habits, I believe we must enjoy the journey. We will not feel the immediate change and growth, and we can lose sight of why we are doing it. This is especially true when it's a big goal that is far into the future because we don't see and feel the daily difference making it harder to stay focused. At work, it's important that we connect feeling better with doing a better job and struggling less to do so to create the change we want.

Can you acknowledge the small steps that each add up to change? We don't get to the top of the mountain by just wanting to get to the top; we get there because we love the climb. It's the process of all our daily choices that creates well-being.

PAUSE ON THIS

- What are the assets and strengths that you want to build on, and what skills do you want to learn?

  _____

  _____

- What drains you and distracts you from your goals and what you care about?

  _____

  _____

- What motivates you and gives or adds to your energy?

  _____

  _____

(continued)

(continued)

- What kind of daily support do you need to stay mindful and motivated?

_____

_____

CHAPTER 13

Self-Expression

"How do I ask for what I need?"

My parents and I were having breakfast, and I could tell my mom was getting increasingly upset about something. I wasn't sure what, and my teenage self was wondering if I had done something wrong. After a few more minutes of noticing her unease and sensing that her anger was clearly rising, I asked her what was going on. "Can't you see I need the jam!" she snapped, "My bread has nothing on it!" I looked at her in surprise. "Sorry, mom, I couldn't tell. Why don't you just ask me to pass the jam?"

We tend to think that other people can see or guess what we need, don't we? We can end up feeling that we don't matter, don't feel seen, respected, or cared about. And we carry that with us if we don't speak up and ask for what we need.

Speaking up is not easy. This is especially true for women. We've traditionally been taught that our role is to take care of others and that social setup is still running today in the under-current of our culture and at work. Sadly, in many countries across the world, this is still the role of the female. Coming from Denmark, where the conversation about equality was already flourishing when I was growing up, provided me with a different mindset. I'm privileged to have been raised in an environment where speaking up is much easier to consider and I was born to a dad who told me I'm equal from the word go. But even with these advantages, I have experienced the struggle to feel heard.

I was in a relationship where, much like the one with my mother, I felt that if I spoke up about who I was, what I needed, or said no when I didn't feel like doing something my partner wanted to do, I'd be in trouble. When I did what I needed to do for me, my partner told me that I wasn't being kind and considerate and that I was being selfish and controlling. When I spoke up, I was told that I was acting like everything was about me and that I didn't have any respect for his needs.

Even when I asked to discuss how we could find a win-win, a way to "Yes, and" about what we each wanted and needed, it wasn't a conversation we could have. The relationship didn't last, but it did leave an impact. It reminded me that if I don't speak up, I'm damaging my mental health and how I self-care. The bottom line is that relationships where we cannot express ourselves tend to leave us doubting our worth and not trusting that we add value. But when we can express ourselves as whole humans and communicate with empathy, we can create trust and navigate change.

Shame at Work

Like many of us, I have been shamed at work for not being strong and resilient enough to pull an all-nighter or for needing to eat lunch. I have been silenced in meetings. I have been talked over, interrupted, and asked to take notes when that was not my job. Even though speaking up is difficult, I invite you to refuse to accept that you are not equally worthy and valued.

You will not always be able to speak up and get your needs met. In some toxic work environments, you might be fired, denied promotions, or otherwise punished for speaking up. In slightly less hostile environments, you might not suffer the same repercussions, but you might feel ignored or not treated seriously. However, it helps to acknowledge for yourself what your needs are, and if possible, communicate them because at least then it doesn't feel quite as much like we are abandoning ourselves. Sometimes it's impossible to be heard, included, cared about, or even respected, but at least we tried, stood up for ourselves, and asked. Sometimes that's all we can do.

I invite you to pause and think about the times when you didn't speak up and what caused this hesitation.

- Did you stay silent because you were trying to keep the peace?

- Did you not speak up because of being bullied and disrespected?

- Did you grow up in an environment where you were told you were needy and to keep your needs to yourself?

You might find that you stay silent far more often than you'd like, hoping to keep the peace because, in the short run, that's easier. Or maybe you don't speak up to fit in, better belong, and feel included. I have consistently heard over the years that people don't express themselves because they don't want to be seen as a troublemaker or difficult. We sacrifice ourselves to be flexible and collaborative at work. We stay silent because we want to be team players. It's not good for our well-being or growth because it reinforces the story we might already be telling ourselves—that we are not good enough and we don't matter. It's also not good for teamwork because your voice is missing.

I often hear people say they shy away from relationships, whether personal or professional, after they have experienced feeling suppressed, shamed, or bullied. What if instead we could think of relationships as where we learn how to support ourselves and ask for what we need? It's okay that we don't get it right; we learn from all of it.

Please don't allow your inner critic to get the best of you here. Turn on your inner coach while using the questions of The Self-Care Mindset® to listen to yourself with the attitude of CARE: curiosity, acknowledgement, respect, and empathy. When we learn to listen with CARE, we learn to engage with empathy, both for ourselves and each other.

This Is Not a Fight; It's Communication

When people I work with start speaking up about what they need, just like with boundaries, they tend to think of it as fighting against and for themselves rather than asking the question, "How do we become more inclusive?"

It makes it harder to speak up when we think of it as a fight, even though a conflict might arise. I recognize that we are socialized to keep the peace and that conflict is not something we learn as being positive and constructive, but it is. Conflict is the path to intimacy between partners, bonding between friends, and an inclusive well-being culture at work. Without conflict, there's no change. Without conflict, there's no diversity. Without conflict, there's no innovation. Without conflict, there's no growth. Without conflict, we are stuck.

In her book, *The Good Fight*, Liane Davey talks about how "conflict debt" gets in the way of progress and describes it as "the sum of all contentious issues that need to be addressed to be able to move forward but instead remain undiscussed and unresolved." So how do we go from thinking it's a fight, to accepting the conflict and embracing communication?

Ask for It

You can use the Self-Care Mindset® principle of asking inclusive questions while focusing on what good would look like rather than the pothole of the conflict.

- What do you need so that you can feel confident asking for what you need?

- What do you need so that you can feel courageous in entering the conflict conversation?

- What do you need so that you can communicate why something matters to you?

- What do you need so that you can be fully self-expressed and belong at work?

- What do you need so that you can embrace who you are?

I'm not going to give you the answers because the whole point is that you learn to listen to yourself. However, I will give you an example of how to work through the first question in the previous list in a way that leans into The Self-Care Mindset®.

What do you need so that you can feel confident in asking for what you need?

- You may need to discuss how you feel with a friend at work and have them confirm that it's within your right to ask for what you need.

- You may need to remind yourself that what you are asking for is a basic human need and nothing extraordinary or outrageous.

- You may need to realize that if you aren't asking for what you need and want, you will stay stuck, and it will hurt both you and your work.

- You may have to remind yourself that no one else knows what you need and might not ask you for it because they are not used to considering how an inclusive well-being culture communicates and asks questions.

Confidence isn't just something we have or find; it takes self-care, which like balancing, is a continued practice of asking questions to adjust and adapt and becoming increasingly agile as we practice. I'm not big on positive affirmations to cultivate confidence. However, if it works for you, go for it. The point is to become mindful of our self-talk. Pausing to listen and notice if we are in the inner critic mindset instead of engaging with the inner coach to feel supported and hold compassion for ourselves as we "go for it."

The inner coach can hold that space for you and reset your focus and attention on what you need to hear right now to support you in feeling confident while being inclusive of how you feel at this time: "I'm capable and able to do this, even if I have my doubts." "What I need right now is to trust myself." "What do I need so that I can trust myself?"

This way, you can keep asking questions that unravel your insecurities and give you more clarity and courage, which is how you gain confidence.

What, How, and Why It Matters

You can only ask for what you need if *you* know what you need and why it matters. And of course, we don't need the same thing all the time. This is why you can think of this as an interactive relationship with yourself that will change, grow, and adapt to different situations and evolve as you start using The Self-Care Mindset® to build better relationships with others too.

I suggest formulating your ask like this: "**I need...because... so that I can....**"

For example, imagine you're feeling irritable and achy because you have been in back-to-back meetings without a chance to get away from the screen. You need to pause to stretch, get some water, and go pee. You have another meeting after this one.

In this situation, you could send an email or text your next meeting and say, "Hey, can we push the meeting 5 minutes? I'm feeling irritable and achy and need to step away to stretch and get some water before we meet so I can be fully present in our conversation. Is that okay with you?"

First, you might inspire someone else to consider their self-care also and encourage them to speak up for what they need. Plus, who will say no when you tell them your reason for doing so is to be more present in the meeting?

Or you could ask if it's okay to make it a walking meeting on the phone. This is a way for both of you to stretch, get outside, and have your meeting without feeling the stickiness that comes from sitting for too long in one go.

Here's another situation where we can choose how we speak up and ask for what we need. Imagine you're headed into a meeting but right before, you learn something has gone wrong with a project you are working on. You start your next meeting by asking for a moment to pause and share that you are feeling distraught, which might affect your attention. You might ask the person if you can share what just happened and ask them if they have any thoughts about what a good next step would be. Or you may ask for the meeting to be moved because you have to get on emails to try to solve it.

It's only fair to the people you are meeting with that you ask for what you need and why it matters to them, so they can make a decision about how they want to engage with you. After all, when given the option, most people will choose you being present over feeling distracted.

The Power of Venting

I'm sure you've gotten caught up in a conversation with someone where they went on and on about someone else and what that person did or said. Or maybe, you have found yourself doing so as well, only to wonder afterward if you should have said what you said.

Some people are concerned that they share too much and come across as if they don't have it together when they may need to talk about it. Where's the balance between transparency, authenticity, communication, and venting?

Even though venting happens when we feel frustrated, it can also be a powerful tool to express ourselves and get valuable feedback that can help us gain clarity.

It can be helpful to set up the parameters for the conversation so it can become an intentional and productive venting session rather than falling into the trap of complaining. This is where Power-Pausing comes in handy so you ensure you communicate what you need from a venting session. You may ask the person to listen or ask for feedback (and specify the kind of feedback you want) after you have let your thoughts loose. I suggest you put a timer on how long you will go on and share that with the person agreeing to the listening session with you.

CARE-Driven Venting

C: **Am I being critical or constructive in my** *communication?*

- Are you only focusing on what's not working and not sharing how you would consider solving the problem?

- Are you getting stuck repeating the same thing?

- Are you guessing what other people are thinking? Or are you focusing on the events, actions, and facts?

A: **Am I being** *aware* **of myself and the person listening to me?**

- What is the venting for? Are you going off on a rant? Or are you asking for the person listening to be a participant by asking for their agreement to hold space for you while you vent?

- Are you trying to get someone to agree with you, or are you just needing to be heard?

- Are you feeling disregarded or disrespected over something? If so, is it your ego trying to get attention? Or is there something you care about that you are trying to figure out how to deal with or get other people to care about too?

- Are you looking for help to find a way forward through something that keeps you stuck and you don't know how to communicate it or who to talk to?

R: Am I taking *responsibility* for my part?

- Are you being honest about why you are venting and being respectful of the person listening by asking them if they are willing to listen and hold space?

- Do you want feedback? Then ask for feedback and listen while they offer you that. It's a gift to have someone listen and then tell you what they heard; however, take responsibility for the feedback you want. Ask them specific questions you would like them to "listen for" while you are sharing your frustration. And let them speak. Don't interrupt.

- If you can tell the person is uncomfortable, take responsibility for how you may come across. Are you being aggressive and angry? Are you ousting people the other person cares about and has to work with? Are you pausing to check-in while venting to make sure you are staying on the topic that you told the person you would like to discuss?

E: Am I *expressing* myself in an honest, transparent, and authentic manner?

- The way we express ourselves must be genuine. Are you simply asking for an audience for emotional venting without pausing to consider how you truly express your emotions? Are you expressing how it's affecting you? Or are you dramatizing it to get sympathy when really what you want is empathy?

- Are you being transparent, honest, and vulnerable in sharing what you are frustrated about, and are you asking for what you need so the person knows how to be there for you?

- Are you telling the whole story without putting yourself on mute because you don't feel safe? If that's the case, you are venting with the wrong person—vent with people you trust so that you can feel psychologically safe to be fully authentic and express your truth.

It takes self-honesty to engage in care-driven conversations. Remember, the person listening is not there to solve your challenges but rather to be a sounding board for you to find your way through the overwhelm and frustration to find clarity, courage, and confidence to speak with the person you need to be speaking with.

Being Authentic

"So being authentic means that I can just fly off the handle and shout at my people? That's what the authentic me would do." I was discussing what "authenticity" means with an executive and how he could be more aware of his emotions to help that be a doorway to better communication with his team.

After sitting with his comment for a moment, I asked him if he considered snapping back to be who he truly was or rather how he reacted when getting upset and frustrated when things weren't going as he wanted. "Yes, I get impatient," he replied while adding what he felt like when the people on his team weren't doing their jobs as he expected them to.

"I'd like you to think about something," I began. "How would you communicate your annoyances if you intended to support your team in working better rather than catching them in doing something wrong?" I asked him to be honest about where his frustration was really coming from.

His eyes met mine when I said this and after some hesitation, he replied, "Are you saying that if I were authentic, I would tell my employees that I was feeling like I'd lost control over the project because they had not done their job?"

"Not quite," I replied. "What I'm suggesting is to recognize how you feel and use that as information to engage better with your employee while being mindful that your intention is to get the project finished. Yelling communicates anger, and it's all about how you feel; however, it doesn't solve any problems and has nothing to do with being authentic."

In the end, he got my point. He was reacting out of emotions rather than integrating how he felt into how he was engaging with his employees in a way that would let the conversation focus on the common goal—getting the project done.

When we CARE, we can use our authenticity to connect, communicate, and collaborate in a way that creates psychological safety. Being authentic isn't about reacting to whatever we feel but rather pausing, listening, and using our authentic emotions as information to make the conversation curious, conscious, and courageous, and with that, we enter the arena of being constructive, creative, and caring all at the same time. Authenticity is how we develop trust, and it takes empathy to get there.

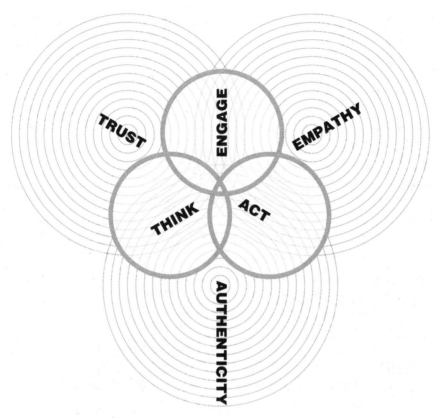

Source: Path For Life®

The Self-Care Mindset® is the link between how we think, engage, and act. I hope that we can all learn to communicate from a place of caring by being aware and inclusive of our own needs, respecting each other, and speaking from a place of healthy boundaries that focus on how we build a Culture of Care® together.

PAUSE ON THIS

- What do you need to support yourself to be able to speak up?

  _____

  _____

- When do you feel you have to hide who you are?

  _____

  _____

- What do you believe is possible if you were to ask for what you need and get the support you need?

  _____

  _____

- Create scenarios for yourself where you ask: I need...so that I can....

  _____

  _____

Becoming You

"Who am I?" It's a question I asked myself for years when I was younger and many of my clients ask it too. We land at this question when we start self-caring because self-care is not about the habits themselves; it's about that deeper relationship we have with ourselves. It's to feel that we belong and fit in by learning to accept ourselves as we are and speak up for what we need by being fully self-expressed. Looking back over my own years of change and growth and seeing how my clients struggle to find themselves, I have learned to embrace that who we are is not a destination; it's a journey fueled by curiosity. Life is about change. We change as kids. We change as teenagers. We change in our 20s; we change in our 30s; we change in our 40s; we change in our 50s, 60s, 70s, and beyond. Can we stay open, listening, curious, and caring throughout? Can we be okay with the fact that life is *not* about getting to a place and calling it a day; it's about learning to be more and more of who we are? Showing up as our whole human amazing selves?

If you are like most people, you might have been told that you have to be something or become someone. You might, like I did, try on different personalities to see which one is going to be accepted, respected, liked, and included the most. And you might get through the process of reading this book, have learned aspects of yourself that you realize have not been allowed to flourish, to show up, and be loved, even by you.

I learned a lot about embracing myself as who I am becoming during menopause. I had to pause and listen to my body with care rather than frustration. Most women struggle with menopause because so much changes in and with us that we can't do what we have always done. For men, there are changes too, and I don't think we talk about that enough either. It's always been a bit hush when changes happen because we feel stuff, and we don't talk about our feelings, do we? At least not at work. But I love aging. I find it fascinating to watch and listen to what my body and my mind need, and I think of it as exploring a new city or even a new country sometimes. I have become more gentle with myself and have become more me. Not dealing with the BS because who has time to waste? My life is waiting for me to be at my best. Yours is too.

In Michelle Obama's book *Becoming*, she takes the journey back to her childhood and with discernment and honesty observes who she was then and how she was constantly *becoming*. She did not set out to become the First Lady, nor did she think of that as her identity and I bet, if you were to ask her today, she's still *becoming*.

We tend to be so hard on ourselves for not being something that aligns with our expectations.

What could change if we could pause for just a moment and appreciate what we have done and who we are becoming?

What if self-care is to understand our worth as the human beings that we are, without the extra bells and whistles that we believe we have to add to be valued?

What if every day we could begin the day curious about what we will learn today, about others, in our work, and about ourselves?

The ego doesn't come from thinking we are great. It comes from not seeing how great we are and trying to boost ourselves to be seen by others. I didn't learn this transformational lesson until I went through loss and grief. That's when I understood what love is, and I could see myself for the human being that I am, the real, honest, vulnerable, and truly powerful me, not because I'm better than, but simply because I understand what it takes to embrace our humanity.

If there's one thing that's for certain, it's that we keep changing and growing. The question is if we are doing it without resisting and embracing who we are continuously becoming.

The four questions of The Self-Care Mindset® will eventually become like a mantra and exercise you can turn to in order to pause, listen, and become intentional about how you use your attention.

1. "Who's thinking, who's talking? Am I my inner critic or my inner coach right now?"

2. "How am I in there?"

3. "What do I need so that I can...?"

4. "How do I ask for what I need?"

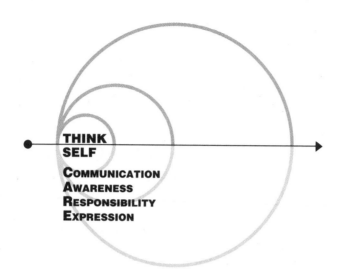

When we reclaim agency over our mind, connect with our heart, and choose how we show up with CARE, we engage with curiosity, acknowledgement, respect, and empathy. We engage in care-driven conversations that are inclusive of our core human needs and cultivate a culture where human beings do better work, together.

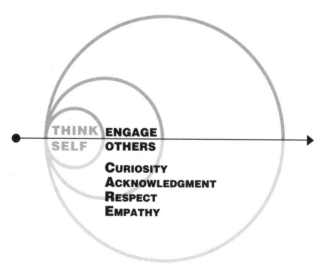

Let's step into Part III of the book where we will harness change and growth by learning how to be more aware, adaptable, and agile so that we can ACT with care.

PART III

ACT—
Reclaiming Agency

CHAPTER 14

ACT with CARE

"Strength doesn't come from ignoring our emotions. Strength comes from using our heart to be in alignment with what we care about."

Growing up in Denmark, my dad and I used to race sailboats. Throughout the summer, we'd plot our tactics and discuss the course only to discover once we headed out onto the ocean that the only thing that was ever predictable was nothing ever being predictable. The weather would change on a dime and affect how we were navigating. The waves and the current would push us sideways, against us, and sometimes with us while we would constantly watch for other boats and what they were doing to ensure we didn't collide. All of this forced us to make fast decisions based on what was happening, not what we had strategized.

Of course, our strategy helped us prepare. However, it was the continued observing and listening to the wind and waves, watching for the constantly changing conditions, and being aware of the other boats that determined how we would adapt our strategy. Our success was determined by our agility, how quickly we could respond, and how willing we were to try something for which we had not planned.

While I watched the other boats and tried to figure out what they might do, my dad was watching the wind and navigating the boat according to our direction. The rest of our three or sometimes four-person team constantly adjusted the sails to optimize the chosen route. Sometimes we got the sails just right after tacking (the term for turning the boat into the wind, shifting the sails to the other side, and changing direction) only to have to tack again because another boat was now on a collision course with us. The key was making a fast decision as to whether we thought it best to hold on and wait or tack right away. While tacking, you are pretty much dead in the water, and it takes a bit to regain momentum and speed so every decision could cost us our position.

I learned a lot about resilience during those years. Being stubborn and screaming and yelling at each other to go faster would not work. Pausing to make better and faster decisions did. We had to trust each other to do our parts and we relied on our communication and the effectiveness of each other to create results.

Today, many people use sailing analogies to illustrate emotional intelligence. But I prefer to use it to showcase resilience. In a sailboat, resilience is to be aware, adaptable, and agile, while having your eye on the goal.

The same applies in the workplace too.

In Part III, ACT, we're going to explore how we reclaim agency and show up at work with more awareness, adaptability, and agility. It's about how we use CARE to make better and faster decisions that align with our goals to survive the future of work and become inclusive of our diverse human needs.

To put this into action, we will dive into our last, and crucial framework, AAA: Acknowledge, Accept, Ask. AAA allows us to be more aware, adaptable, and agile when facing our own challenges as well as when communicating with others, while redefining what it means to be resilient.

AAA: Resilience from the Inside Out

Even though the world has changed, our concept of resilience hasn't as we still view it as shutting up, biting down, and keeping going no matter what while keeping our emotions to ourselves. At work, this shows up as pushing through without breaks between meetings, not having time for lunch, and waiting till the end of the day, the weekends, or declaring "self-care" days to take care of ourselves and recharge. In short, it's what we view as being tough.

But being tough is not being strong.

Strong is acknowledging how we feel and using our self-awareness to listen to the FUD (fear, uncertainty, doubt) as it arises and choosing to focus on what we can control. It's about accepting *what is* so we can be adaptable in having difficult conversations, ask what we need so that we can make hard decisions, own how we show up, and harness agility.

Like the sailing example, I view resilience as being in relationship with *what is* and using it to inform our next step, next choice, or in-action. What does it mean to be in a relationship with *what is?* It's pausing to listen to yourself, asking forward-focused questions, and aligning with the outcome you are steering toward.

For me, this looks a lot like operating from a place of flow, which is often referred to as "being in the zone," where we are fully present in the moment. In this case, I think of flow as the power of water. It's the softest, yet most powerful substance; it's the most relentless because it's adaptable and agile; it's the stillest and strongest. Water constantly changes in relation to the environment, conditions, time of day, typography, landscape, and weather.

In the same regard, we are steady and stable in who we are when we lean into The Self-Care Mindset®. It allows us to know ourselves better and act in flow with the circumstances and the problems we are facing while making choices in the direction of the solution we want to achieve. When we are aware, we can be more adaptable and agile, and that's how we are resilient. So rather than shutting up and pushing through, I developed AAA as a tool to turn FUD into action.

- In the "Acknowledge" stage, we ask ourselves, "How am I in there?"

- In the "Accept" stage, we face the reality of *what is.*

- In the "Ask" stage, we ask ourselves, "What do I need so that I can?"

AAA is my favorite quick tool. It has the power to help you think in a way that allows you to get unstuck and make faster decisions, which we are going to focus on in this chapter before exploring how we can also use AAA to communicate with others to engage and collaborate with care in Chapter 15, "Yes, And... Is There More?"

We've gone through how to ask ourselves "How am I in there?" and "What do I need so that I can?" throughout the course of this book. Now we're going to gain the tools to *accept* the circumstances in front of us based on what they are because acceptance is the key to moving from resistance to resilience and ultimately, harness change and grow.

AAA
ACKNOWLEDGE, ACCEPT, ASK

ACCEPT: THE SITUATION FOR WHAT IT IS.
DON'T WASTE TIME WISHING IT WAS DIFFERENT.

ACKNOWLEDGE:
PAUSE & ASK YOURSELF,
HOW AM I IN THERE
RIGHT NOW AND HOW
DO I FEEL?

ASK: WHAT DO I NEED
SO THAT I CAN...?

Acceptance and Reclaiming Agency

"We cannot change what has happened; it's in the past. We cannot control what will happen; it's in the future. We can only be in relationship with the present moment; it's the only one we have agency over how we respond to what is." - Dalai Lama

A recent client was having a hard time accepting mistakes she had made, and with that, the circumstances she was in. She was stuck, arguing for why something should not have happened and how it was now stopping her from achieving her goals. She insisted that she had no power over what had happened and that since she couldn't change it, she felt lost and powerless. She wanted the mistake to not have happened.

To give her an example of adaptability to changing circumstances, I asked her how she responds if it starts to rain. I figured that would help her see what I meant by accepting the circumstances for what they are and making decisions based on that. But her answer surprised me, which explained why she was so stuck. "I want it to stop raining," she said. "I hate the rain." Grabbing an umbrella and a raincoat was not an option for her, only stopping the rain from happening was. This shows the mindset that keeps us stuck when change happens and we burn out. Instead of learning to surf the waves of life, we keep swimming against the tide.

At work, we often get stuck in meetings or in our own thoughts discussing why and how something happened; a mistake on the budget, a decision that didn't pay off, a comment we made and regretted, a presentation where we didn't include the key argument and the client didn't go with it, or an interview where we didn't perform well. Every day we will be in situations where we made a choice that didn't work out the way we intent or expect.

We humans project stories of things that went wrong in the past and imagine that's what will happen again in the future. Cy Wakeman is a drama researcher, thought-leader, and author recognized for her counterintuitive perspective on reality-based leadership, and she says we lose 2.5 hours a day in the drama of our own minds resisting and arguing with reality.

To remedy this, we need to recognize the power in accepting *what is*. It's how we create change and grow, harness motivation, meet the FUD face to face, and come together for what we believe in. Wishing it were different is about resisting what has happened, instead of using it to create the change we want to see.

As my dad and I were approaching the day where we'd have to say goodbye to each other, I learned a lot about the power of accepting *what is* to give me the agency to navigate the future without him and also enjoy the time I had left with him. Yes, we grieved together that he was dying. We talked about regret and how he wished he had traveled more and how things would maybe have turned out differently if he hadn't taken a month off from treatment to spend time with my mom while she was going through her treatment in Denmark.

But we could not change reality. So we acknowledged that's how we felt but we did not waste any time dwelling on it. We asked ourselves, "What do we need so that we can make this time we have left together precious, remarkable, and a time together that would prepare me for being alone?"

Accepting he was dying was accepting a very difficult, deeply sad, infuriating, and helpless fact. But it gave us back the power and agency to spend our last few months together in a meaningful way. It gave us agency to focus on healing the pain of this fact together. Once we had aired and shared how we felt to each other, we could spend all our time together, making what was left of it something that mattered.

In the beginning, I was scared. We both were. We did not know what the dying process would be like. I asked a teacher and old mentor of mine to come speak with us about the dying process so that we could be prepared, and it came in handy many times when I had to remind my dad to accept the process. After he died, I was at peace because we had already spent so much time preparing for that moment and it allowed me to better adapt to the uncertainty of life that awaited me once he passed.

It was a difficult time and a challenging lesson to learn, but it gave me a life-altering insight: It takes awareness to accept ourselves, acceptance of our circumstances to become adaptable, and adaptability to become agile in how we approach life and work.

The Power of Being Aware, Adaptable, and Agile

General Motors CEO Mary Barra is a solution-oriented and transformative thinker. She credits her success on her ability to focus on finding the way forward rather than getting stuck in the potholes of life. That's the essence of resilience that comes from accepting the situation and doing what you can—with what you have—to make the best of it.

The power of adaptability is the power to listen. Not to the thoughts in our own mind that might tell us that something unforeseeable just happened and now we are in trouble, but instead having the ability to recognize change for what it is. We often get stuck because we pursue the expectations we had set, and when change happens, the FUD can kick in and we try to solve the wrong problem, the one that created change.

The ability to pause and revisit how we reach our expectations or if we need to calibrate them to navigate what is, is the power of making better decisions. Take the example of getting stuck in a pothole when driving. You are not going to spend much time discussing how you landed there because that's not solving the problem. You are going to accept that you landed there and figure out how to get your car out of the hole. Fast. This is the thing about speed; it comes from adaptability, not just pushing harder.

Using AAA as a tool, we use our ability to change and grow by *acknowledging* how we feel, *accepting* the circumstances for what it is, and then *asking* what we need, so that we can navigate and harness the challenges ahead.

That's the true definition of resilience as it allows us to recover from disappointment, reclaim agency over the situation, and act faster to make a decision, solve a problem, or change direction. It's also how we access our creativity and innovation because we avoid the potholes and reclaim agency over our decisions.

Many of us start out the day in tension, worried about what problems may arise. In my retail days, as discussed in Chapter 7, I originally viewed problems as a disruption to my day that kept me away from my "to-do" list. What I realized, though, was my entire job (and the very reason the job was created) was to solve the problems my team faced and my customers experienced. Through this switch of expecting problems to arise instead of fearing them, my stress levels completely changed. I delegated my to-do list, which made my team members feel more included while increasing their agency. We all changed our perspective to being problem-solvers and I became the coach of my team. We all not only grew together, but so did our sales numbers and our customer satisfaction as we brought a lot more joy to our work.

Today, when I meet a problem, I use AAA as a method to work through it. My mind is more productive about what I'm focused on achieving and helps me be in flow rather than stuck in the rehashing of what's not working.

AAA with Care

Working with CARE, we can use AAA to recognize that what we care about is what drives us. In the process of checking in with ourselves, the door opens for us to ask, "Does it matter?"

It's easy to get confused by FUD and let the fear distract us from what we care about. However, fear is the sibling of what we care about, so pause for just a little longer to use AAA to connect with care. For example, if you say to yourself, "I'm scared that I'm going to lose my job," it's crucial to then ask yourself, "Why does it matter?" This leads you to think about how much you care about supporting yourself, your family, paying your bills, and keeping your home, which are all good motivators to move forward.

To see this in action, you can now use AAA this way:

- **Acknowledge:** "I'm scared I will lose my job."

- **Accept:** "If I were to lose my job...," use a statement that accepts the problem rather than worrying about the problem.

- **Ask:** "What do I need so that I can support myself and my family, pay my bills, and keep my home?"

An executive wanted to discuss a difficult decision that she was facing. She was no longer thriving in her career and had been offered a new position, which required her to change from working remotely at home to working full-time at the office, which meant her family would have to relocate. Using the AAA tool, here's the process we went through, which helped her gain clarity on the decision that had to be made.

- **Acknowledge how the person feels:** Even though she had a good relationship with her boss, she felt there was no longer room for growth and felt micro-managed. I asked if she felt that was a problem that could be solved, and she didn't feel it was.

  She shared how anxious she was about considering new opportunities, and as a coping mechanism, she talked herself into feeling excited about it. But instead of glossing over the anxiety, I asked her if we could pause on the anxiety and use it to understand what she needed to make a decision that she felt confident about.

- **Accept the situation for what it is:** The idea of moving was overwhelming. First, the increased cost of living in a new location. Second, the family loved the community they lived in and would not want to permanently move to another location. Third, they wanted to keep the current house and would have to either rent it out or be able to afford two places. And of course, everyone would have to relocate and settle into a new environment.

- **Ask "What do you need so that you can make a decision that works for your needs and lifestyle?":** After exploring what she would need to accept the job, it became clear that having to move her family was not something she was willing to do. She felt confident in telling the company that she would need to work remotely and travel to the office when needed if they wanted her to accept the position. In the end, the company presented her an offer beyond what she had imagined she would receive.

Using AAA to walk through each scenario that she had to consider helped her get clear about the nuances that often get us stuck in feeling overwhelmed when feeling anxious about change. Instead of dismissing the anxiety and telling ourselves we "should" be excited, we can pause to explore what we need to feel confident about embarking on the change, feel calm about saying "not now," or ask for what we need.

Simply put, AAA gives you back the power of choice and your voice. You can now start being curious and ask for what you need to feel secure and happy so that you can fuel your performance and build your resilience from the inside out.

AAA not only works for professional challenges, but personal ones as well. I recently went through surgery for skin cancer under my eye. I was not concerned about the cancer itself as it wasn't the invasive kind. But I was concerned about the potential size of the scar it would leave and people looking at it when we interacted. Here's how I used AAA to stay calm and focused.

- **Acknowledge:** I was concerned about the impact it would have on my face and how long I might have a very visible scar.

- **Accept:** I accepted that I would not know the impact of the surgery until after it was done. I also knew and accepted that I would need reconstructive surgery. Again, I would not know the impact until the day of.

- **Ask:** "What do I need so that I can be prepared to heal *after* the surgery is done?" In this way I could *suspend worry* and focus on getting myself set up to take really good care of myself for the somewhat unforeseeable time it would take.

AAA on Purpose

When most people hear the word "purpose," they think about what they are meant to do and if they are living their purpose. But I invite you to also think about if in each moment, you are acting with purpose based on what you are working to achieve right now.

When I go on stage it might be aligned with my higher purpose to facilitate change in the workplace so we can live better lives through self-care. But in the moment, my purpose is to ensure each member of the audience has a good time and receives my message in the most aspirational and actionable way. Achieving this gives them the tools to immediately start to better navigate change and create growth in the areas that matter to them.

Of course, this may sound great. But it isn't always easy. No matter what is going on in my life, when I'm on stage, the audience has to be the focus. AAA helps with that and moves me from being nervous, where I'm focusing on myself, to excited, where I'm focusing on them—the audience—and asking myself what they might need so that they can better harness their well-being. It's the difference between being in tension and using my intention to focus on what matters.

We all have different stressors and when in high-stress conditions, I invite you to align yourself with what your purpose is right now. Embrace AAA by acknowledging the circumstances, accept them for *what is*, and ask yourself what you need so that you can better navigate the pothole in front of you to accomplish the outcome you are looking to achieve with clarity, confidence, and courage.

I ask you to recognize how powerful you are when you care. Please know that when you worry, it's because you care. And you can shift your attention back to what you care about and ask yourself what you need so that you can keep your focus and attention on what matters.

PAUSE ON THIS

- What are situations where you typically "toughen up" to be resilient and then compare that to when you pause before taking action?

_____

_____

- What are typical situations where you react fast and instead could use AAA to pause and respond with care and on purpose? This could be in meetings where you rush to answer because you feel insecure, or when a team member comes to you with a problem and you tell them how to fix it. It could also be a way you react when you are told that something is wrong with your work, and you start defending it instead of pausing and using AAA to explore what you can do to make it right.

_____

_____

CHAPTER 15

"Yes, And…Is There More?"

"We can 'Yes, but' someone to burnout or we can 'Yes, and' someone to growth."

Do you believe in four-leaf clovers? I do. Sometimes I set out to look for them and sometimes I stumble upon them when I'm out and about. When I ask people if they believe in them, it's not so much about the four-leaf clovers as it is what they represent and the exercise of looking for something that might or might not be there. That sense of not-knowing can spark curiosity, creativity, and constructive thinking.

When we are operating in a place of FUD though, it's much harder to access that uncomfortable space between knowing and not knowing. The problem for many people, including leaders and organizations, is to spark an environment where not knowing is a positive and encouraging space to work in, where learning is the foundation for innovation, change, and growth.

What does that have to do with four-leaf clovers? We only look for what we believe is possible, and when we have an attitude of already knowing, we look for proof that we are right rather than looking for what can change.

I recently heard Michael Ciannilli, program manager for the Apollo Challenger Columbia Lessons Learned Program at the Kennedy Space Center, talk about lack of imagination as the problem that can cause mistakes when working under pressure. He pointed to the need to pause and listen more closely to avoid fatal mistakes, like the crash of the Challenger in 1986. Had they paused to listen more instead of rushing to launch, they might have been able to imagine what could go wrong with just a small O-ring, which had been flagged by Allan McDonald, the engineer who refused to sign off on the recommendation to launch. Just an O-ring, easily pushed aside and ignored, with a big impact that cost lives.

Are we willing to open up, not know, and learn? Are we willing to not be right? Are we willing to imagine more and try something when we don't know if it's going to work? Are we willing to keep looking even if we don't find what we are seeking right away? Are we willing to stay curious and listen for just a little longer?

I'm using the example of the four-leaf clovers to illustrate what it means to have a growth mindset. When I'm looking for clovers, I often don't just find one; I often find several. I've even found five-leaf clovers on several occasions. And believe it or not, I once wondered if six-leaf clovers exist, and as soon as I did, I found one. Now, that may seem like magic, and it sure felt like it at the time. The most exciting thing about it was that it was right outside my own front door. To think that this six-leaf clover had been right there under my nose by the time I paused to wonder if it were possible.

We tend to be "Yes, but-ers" in our daily busy lives. However, "Yes, but" negates what we have just said, basically saying it's not valid while dismissing new ideas. This is especially true when we are trying to be all-knowing and prove that we are right about something. We become dismissive. We become closed-minded. And we stop looking to see if there's more. We "Yes, but" and argue for why we are right and someone else is wrong, instead of saying, "Yes, and... is there more?" "Yes, and what about this? Or this? And this...?"

There's a little-known fact that when we find one four-leaf clover, there's often more in the same area. However, we tend to be satisfied when we find the first one, and we run with it. In the same way, we tend to solve the problem with the first idea we get rather than pausing to ask, "Is there more?"

"Yes, and..." Building on Your Strengths

When talking about growth, I'm not just talking about growth as more and faster, as I think of growth as accessing what makes us better. To build on our strengths and become more inclusive we need to become "Yes, and-ers!"

"Yes, and" is popular in improv circles. When one person says something, the next person has to build on what that person said by saying "Yes, and..." and then go from there. For example:

- The first person may say something like: "I took my dog for a walk, and when I got into the street I noticed I still had my slippers on...."

- And then the second person would build on that with something like, "Yes, and when I noticed I still had my slippers on, I decided to keep walking to see if anyone would notice. When I got to the corner...."

- And then the third person would build on that with something like, "Yes, and when I got to the corner it started raining, so my dog and I went for cover under a tree. After about 15 minutes of standing there...."

- Now you keep going, building on this with your imagination.

So what does this have to do with building on our strengths? When we "Yes, and..." we are inclusive of *what is* rather than rejecting *what is* by saying "Yes, but...."

Say the phrases below out loud and think about the difference you feel. "I'm working hard *but* I have to work harder," and "I'm working hard *and* I have to work harder." Or "I'm nervous about the presentation *but* I have to make it happen," and "I'm nervous about the presentation *and* I have to make it happen."

In the first sentences, when we say "but," we are dismissing what was just said. That's what *but's* do. Sometimes that works. But when we want to be inclusive and build on our strengths, we want to become "Yes, and-ers."

- "I'm working really hard on the presentation because I'm nervous about it, *and* I have to make it happen. So what do I need so that I can do that?"

- "That's a great idea, I can tell you are excited about it, *and* what about how it affects our clients? What do you need so that we can explore that?"

In these sentences, we are building on "what is" rather than *what is not*. We are taking the approach of acknowledging the circumstances and the challenges—aka the potholes—*and* we are asking what we need so that we can keep moving in the direction we are going.

A mentor of mine always said, "Instead of catching people in what they are doing wrong, catch people in what they are doing right." That's what being a "Yes, and-er" is all about.

"Yes, and..." AAA as a Communication Tool

When engaging with others, you can use AAA to cultivate better connection, communication, and collaboration. It is a tool for empathetic listening and engagement. Leaders tell me they are burning out, partly from the pressure that's on them to constantly navigate a changing work environment, care about their teams, and continue to be productive. AAA is not only a great tool for us to get unstuck and be inclusive of our self-care and what we need so that we can keep navigating change, care, and be productive, it's a new language that we can use together to create more care-driven work environments and conversations.

I shared this tool with an executive who was going into a performance review with a team member. She was concerned with how to best communicate that the team member's performance was lacking, and if there was no change, she would be fired. Part of the challenge for my client was that she had promoted this person into the job that she was failing in and not just that, she actually believed the woman was more than capable and up for the role, but it just wasn't working.

I asked her if we could pause on one crucial fact, *"that she actually believed the person was capable,"* and I asked a few more questions about that. She explained how she really liked the team member and thought she would be able to do the job and was confused why she wasn't performing. She started discussing what she thought might be the problem, which essentially comes down to guessing what's inside someone else's head and heart.

To set the communication, I used AAA when asking her questions and summed up what I heard:

- **Acknowledge:** You feel uncomfortable about going into this performance meeting because you really like this person, you think she's capable, and you promoted her so you also feel it would be a failure on your part to have to let her go.

- **Accept:** She's not performing to your expectations, and you will have to let her go if that doesn't change.

- **Ask:** What do you need to feel comfortable having a heart-to-heart conversation with her?

Using AAA, this is how I suggested approaching the conversation:

- **Acknowledge** that you see her as perfectly capable to do the job you promoted her to do and you want to see her succeed.

- Make it clear that the situation we need to **accept** is that she's not performing to expectations.

- **Ask** her what she is struggling with and what she needs so that she can work better and perform the job.

They ended up having a great conversation about what was getting in the way. Her team member started crying and released so much of the pressure she had been under, sharing how her old boss had never told her that she was appreciated or a valued member of the team. And then she added, "No one had ever asked me what I needed so that I could perform better." It developed into a constructive and supportive performance review where she could share her obstacles and it gave her back agency to ask for the help she needed to perform better.

The most simple question is also the most powerful and easy to use with yourself and the people you lead: *"What do you need so that you can...?"*

The executive in this story later shared with me that she has that question on a sticky note on her computer screen, and it has changed how she thinks and engages with her people, and it's helping everyone reclaim agency and make better decisions.

I teach this model to companies I speak at, and I often get feedback on how that simple question creates momentum. I heard from a leader who shared it with their young nephew who was a new manager. He started using it and it completely changed how he was working with his team. Sometimes we just need to pause, listen, and ask better questions to align with our goals and engage with the people we lead to do the same.

On that note, here's a deeper look into how you would use the AAA tool in communication:

- **Acknowledge:** Pause to bring awareness to how you feel so that you can be fully present. Recognize what's *yours* to deal with. What I mean is, if you are feeling impatient or irritable, don't snap at the person you are engaging with and instead, leave *what's yours to be yours*. We often project how we think and feel onto others, so if we are feeling insecure about something, we might project onto them that they are over-powering. We also listen with the filter of our own emotions, perceptions, and objectives. To acknowledge how someone is feeling or thinking, make sure you are indeed listening to the person and what they are facing and helping them see their way through it by holding space for them.

- **Accept:** We need empathy. It's an important part of culti-vating better conversations, especially with someone who's struggling with a situation, be it something that's happen-ing, has happened, a mistake they made, or a challenge that they are facing. Empathy, however, is not sympathy or telling someone they will be fine and that they are strong in an attempt to try to cheer them on to keep going. All of that comes from a great place of care; however, helping someone through something is to hold a space of listening for them. Helping them accept the situation rather than trying to fix it. Even if it's easy to fall into the trap of wanting the person to feel better, it's often more about our own discomfort that we jump in with a solution. So often I hear stories about how someone is not feeling heard or seen because the person they are confiding in is telling them what they think they should think, feel, and do in a situation where they are having a hard time. Sometimes we just need to allow for a pause to simply accept the situation so that we can move on.

In a conversation where we focus on accepting things as they are, we can simply say "yes" when someone is telling us what's gone wrong or what's not working. Remember, it's easy to get stuck in what's not working, especially when we are under stress, which is often the case when things go wrong at work.

A CEO once told me that the strongest way we can show up is by admitting what we don't know, or that we've made a mistake. Mistakes are a *missed take* of a situation. If we make a mistake once, it's either not having enough information or we try something out that doesn't work. Many organizations are talking about having a culture where it's okay to fail and yet, are we accepting when it doesn't work out?

The mistakes we tend to harp over the most are the ones where we are rushed and simply didn't pause to listen, pay attention, and ask more questions before acting. These are also the ones we tend to feel most shame and blame over, which is why empathy when listening and "Yes, and-ing" is so crucial in helping someone move through it to the next point.

- **Ask:** "What do you need so that you can...*for whatever it is the person you are communicating with is working to solve?*" You can think of this as the coaching approach to communication and leadership. Instead of giving someone all your good ideas of what you think they should do, use AAA to help them find their own way forward.

Let's look at another example to see this in action:

- **Person 1:** "I have so much work and I cannot get it all done. I'm exhausted and feel like I'm burning out. I'm not sure how much longer I can hold out, and this project is so important. I need a break and there isn't one coming anytime soon."

- **Person 2:** "I understand that you are exhausted and feel like you cannot keep going much longer. This project is very important and is asking a lot of you. Since the project isn't over anytime soon, instead of waiting till this is behind you, what do you need so that you can self-care more throughout the day to get some pauses to recover your energy and reclaim your focus here and there?"

This way we are talking about how to better manage our energy instead of wishing the project wasn't taking so long and asking so much of us. It's a small shift in focus. But it has a big impact. This is how we start solving the right problem: managing our energy so that we can get through the project rather than trying to figure out how to avoid doing the work required to make it a great project.

We all fall into the trap of cutting corners instead of pausing to ask what we need so we can self-care for the long haul. The key, however, is to begin to catch ourselves in order to have more constructive conversations with ourselves and others.

Let's look at another example that may be relatable to you:

Person 1: "I feel so anxious and stressed. I made a mistake on the budget, and my manager will be furious when she finds out because she is headed into a meeting soon."

The person is under stress and very possibly in either flight, fight, or freeze mode. This means we default to stress behaviors: trying to avoid owning up to the mistake and blaming it on something or someone else, defending it, or simply just stuck, feeling paralyzed in anxiety and stress, and repeating the same over and over, hoping it's not going to be discovered. Neither situation solves the problem: The manager is headed into a meeting.

Person 2: "I understand you are feeling anxious and stressed about having made a mistake on the budget. Since your manager already has the budget and is headed into a meeting to present it, what do you need so that you can minimize the effect this might have?"

The person might need to be backed up to have the confidence to own up before his manager goes into the meeting for example. It takes a little practice to learn to "Yes, and" in conversations, so practice it with everyday situations like figuring out dinner plans and such.

A Healthy Culture Is Built on Healthy Conversations

The point is to raise each other up by being inclusive of how others feel and use it as information to guide us to the solution. This is the same as cultivating better conversations with ourselves and why self-care helps us be aware, pay attention, listen, and care better about each other.

We want to be helpful. However, that tends to be how we end up diminishing how someone feels by saying it will be okay, they can handle it, they will figure it out, and we leave them hanging to do so on their own, only to get stuck in FUD. Or we rush to tell them what to do about it without asking them what they think could work. To become coaches to each other is the most productive kind of care-driven conversation we can have. And it works with kids too. My dad used coaching questions when I was growing up and it taught me how to think better; it gave me the confidence to solve my own problems and the independence to take charge. In the same way, we see how leaders need to become coaches to be the kind of leaders that we need right now.

The role of the leader has changed; it's no longer about managing the project but rather supporting their people in managing their energy, focus, and attention so they can do their best work.

People at work want to feel like they matter, they want to have agency, and they want to reclaim their personal and professional growth. They also want to feel that their work and their lives are synthesized into being whole human beings. The reality is we have always felt this way, and COVID gave us the opportunity to rethink the way we work so that being human is indeed the advantage we harness.

Loss of agency and feeling like our ideas, thoughts, and options don't matter causes burnout and leads to people leaving their jobs in search of a place where they feel appreciated for who they are and can grow by building on their strengths.

To do so we need to foster a culture where, instead of suppressing our feelings, we give people back agency to co-create solutions. This is all a work in progress for people and companies together, To build a healthy work culture together we need to cultivate an environment where we can talk about it and that includes how we feel and how we would like to handle things.

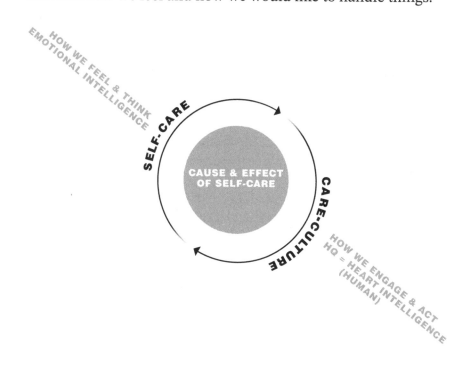

PAUSE ON THIS

- When are the times you find yourself waiting to share your opinion rather than pausing to truly listen to someone to understand where they are coming from?

  _____

  _____

- When are the times you stop yourself from sharing your opinion because you think your perspective is not important?

  _____

  _____

- When are the times you could "Yes, and" more in conversations to include different perspectives and diverse opinions before rushing to a conclusion?

  _____

  _____

CHAPTER 16

From Me to We

"We don't self-care alone; it's how we work better together."

Did you know that trees talk to each other? It may not be like the chatter in a room full of people. But trees have an underground relationship and scientists have learned that they connect, communicate, and collaborate through their root system to support each other's growth.

Just like culture, trees are an ecosystem. And even if we just see each of them individually, none of them exists on their own.

Neither do we.

Culture Is an Ecosystem

Culture is an ecosystem that exists whether or not we pay attention to it. It's the atmosphere. It's the undercurrent. It's the conversations. And we are all part of this ecosystem because it's built on the relationships among us.

Many people think of culture as the "designer environment," and it was when it consisted of artisanal coffee and beer on tap. The ping-pong tables and community areas created a fun culture, at least on the surface. In this sense, we could "see" culture, and it looked a lot like a physical place. But that all went away with COVID, and we had to pause and really learn what creates a healthy culture.

Culture isn't about the benefits, rewards, or perks; it's about the people and the relationships we have. For many people today, work is their community. Some even say, "We are like family." However, I think of that as adding unconscious, though not deliberate, pressure on people because the roles that we have in our family are not the same roles that we want to fit into at work. I understand the intent is to say we care and trust each other, so instead, let's ask, "How do we cultivate that?"

The community or culture at work is built on the relationships between us, which emerge from the way we engage and communicate with each other. There is always culture. The question is, what is it like?

Everything is interconnected. Everything is a relationship. And everything interacts with and affects each other. When you walk into a room, you feel something. It may be the decor, the lights, the smell, or the people that affect you. Even if no words are spoken, there's an atmosphere, a feeling in the room, isn't there? When we walk into a room where people have just argued, we can tell, right? We can also tell when we walk into a room where people are happy and care about each other.

You might need to pause to notice it, but we are in constant communication with our surroundings, each other, and ourselves too as our body regulates and responds based on our circumstances and surroundings. Your heart starts beating faster when you sense danger; your body temperature goes up or down to regulate and adjust to the environment you are in. We don't normally think of our daily lives in this way, but that's how both stress and well-being are contagious. I bet you feel the difference between being inside an office or outside in nature. I'm sure you have been in meetings where you get the sense that you best not say anything and other meetings where you feel welcome and that you belong. How do we understand psychological safety, belonging, and inclusion so that we can consciously work with it in a constructive and collaborative way?

Many of us have been changing jobs and onboarding during COVID. At this point, some of us may have finally had the opportunity to meet our co-workers face-to-face while others continue a virtual relationship. Many who used to work in the field, traveling to customers, had to rethink their client interactions and relationships and learn how to maintain the connection in a new setting. If you think back to those first awkward moments, the continued effort to stay connected, and how you feel now about meeting people in person again, can you recognize that you have a lot of thoughts, feelings, and emotions about it? Can you also recognize that how you feel affects how you interact and show up in those relationships? We may not have thought about this much in the past, but it's now the focus of the conversation about the future of work.

The question we need to solve for the future of work to work better for us is: How do we foster the human connection that we have learned from the impact of the pandemic that is so important for our mental health and essential for thriving at work?

Was Maslow Wrong?

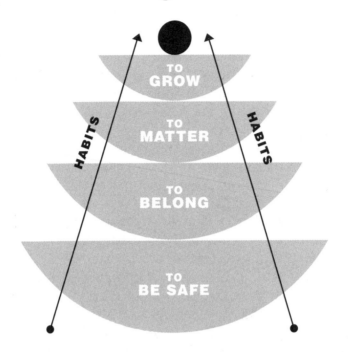

Maslow's hierarchy of needs tells us that the goal of self-care is to self-actualize. So, it's no surprise we think it's all about us as individuals. The whole model of growth is based on fulfilling our needs for physical safety, emotional connection, and social respect before finally self-actualizing. It's a very me, me, me approach to growth and one of the reasons why there's a social stigma around self-care and also possibly why it feels lonely to climb the proverbial ladder at work. Since Maslow's work on our human needs was published, we have seen some changes in how we understand what helps us thrive and grow.

It's not a secret that many of us are no longer choosing the jobs and companies that pay the most and have the most rewards. Many of us today want something different, something more. We want to work for places that foster trust and belonging, where we can grow and have agency in our work. Essentially, we are choosing our futures based on where we trust that we will feel cared about. The collective culture versus the individualistic culture is shifting our concept of self and the way we thrive through our interaction with others is key to our emotional, mental, and even physical health.

Psychologist Carl Rogers speaks about the three components of "who I am" as self-image, ideal self, and self-esteem and how our environment and the people we engage with affect these concepts of self. So you can see how "me and we" is interconnected and why a healthy culture is not just a "nice to have" but essential for creating workplaces where people want to work—or should I say, spend their lives.

According to McKinsey, nearly two-thirds of US-based employees surveyed said that COVID-19 has caused them to reflect on their purpose in life. And nearly half said that they are reconsidering the kind of work they do because of the pandemic. Millennials were three times more likely than others to say that they were reevaluating work. The research found that 70 percent of employees said that their sense of purpose is defined by their work. No wonder we need work to work better for us, and culture is a key management strategy in the future of work.

Marcus Buckingham, head of people and performance research at ADPRI, shared in his recent book, *Love + Work*, that when organizations invest in weekly check-ins with their people, they see team members' engagement increase by 77 percent, while people who trusted their teammates, their leader, and their senior leaders were 15 times more engaged and 42 times more resilient.

It's clear that our whole human health and our self-care is no longer a personal problem but rather a company culture possibility.

We Need Each Other

We need each other and we need to feel cared about. Looking at how various cultures and communities have survived throughout history, it's the strength of the community that's important.

When I studied mind-body-social health, we looked at trauma and its impact on our core needs for belonging to a community to feel safe. Rather than understanding the story of what happened, the focus is on the more inherent cause and effect of feeling excluded, loss of psychological safety, and separation from the community as the key to surviving trauma. The essential shift in how we see Maslow's hierarchy of needs is that food on the table and shelter are not the primary danger to our survival; being outside of the community is. In our modern life, where many live separate from family, our work has become that community.

With clients, I see the need for the emotional and psychological safety that comes from inclusion and belonging as a key factor in self-care. When we don't feel we matter and when we don't feel seen and heard, we feel excluded from the community and end up not feeling that we matter, including to ourselves. When we don't feel we contribute and are important in the context of the whole, we don't self-care. In fact, we do the opposite as we tend to self-abuse instead with too much food, alcohol, work, and TV. We try to numb the pain, the heartache of not belonging. It's not surprising; we are social beings and inspire self-worth in each other simply by caring. It's the reality of how interconnected we are and why self-care works better together.

It's the human connection that's the key. Not only to unlock self-care but to build a strong culture where people belong and work better together. The interactive crux of this is that we can only connect to others to the level we are able to connect to ourselves. Buddhist philosophy teaches us that we feel more engaged and worthy when we are in the service of others; however, they preface that it starts with our connection with self. In her book *Atlas of the Heart*, Brené Brown shares how new data have come out that supports exactly that. We can only connect with others to the extent that we are able to connect with ourselves.

Self-Care Works Better Together

This is why we need to rethink self-care from ME to WE and recognize the power of self-care at work. When self-care is at the center of our three core relationships (with ourselves, work, and each other), we can harness the ripple effect of care and cultivate a work environment that opens up the human connection, allowing us to feel like we matter and belong. This isn't because we shift our identity to adapt to others though, but because we express ourselves authentically.

So instead, I challenge you to turn Maslow's hierarchy of needs upside down.

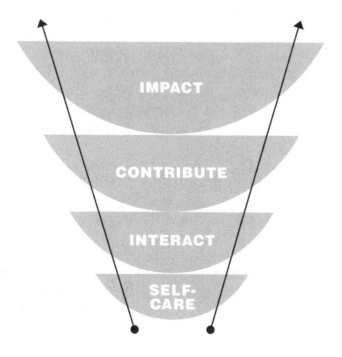

With self-care as the foundation for cultivating a better relationship with ourselves, it affects how we engage with others, and with that, how we create impact together. You can think of it as the cause and effect of The Self-Care Mindset®. It helps us connect better with ourselves so that we connect and communicate better with others, and with that, collaborate better with others to pursue what we care about.

When I was working for Esprit, it was mandatory to stop for lunch every day and go to the cafeteria together where a chef served delicious, healthy food. It was not only mandatory because they wanted us to eat healthier food, but also because of the conversations that were shared during lunch. Sure, sometimes we talked about work. But most of the time we didn't. I have never seen teams be there for each other and help each other the way we did at Esprit.

Eating together builds trust and forms bonds. The NBA's most-winning coach, Gregg Popovich, credits the strong cultures and bonds he built to focusing on nourishing the human connection. He was known for making sure his teams had meals together as often as possible. One other crucial aspect of his coaching was asking questions, creating inclusivity, creating space for contribution, and giving back agency to the team. That's the foundation for thriving. It's the key that unlocks a healthy culture. And it starts with the relationship we have with ourselves because it's the same mindset that gives us the framework to engage better and show up stronger together.

The challenge at work today is that we are navigating a hybrid work environment, and we are trying to figure out how to maintain the human connection that fuels culture. There's a big difference between seeing culture as a group of individuals or team energy and how strong that is as a whole. Sometimes people go along with the group to belong and fit in. That's not a connected culture; that's a toxic one. Culture is about the individual as a part of the collective, contributing, engaging, and showing up with trust and transparency where they lead with curiosity, compassion, commitment, and the courage to be who they are. Getting to the point where we can do that takes self-care.

We have a lot of work to do to truly harness the human advantage so that we can create a strong and safe culture. But we have to, because that's what we need from the future of work to be happy and healthy. And it's what companies need to not only keep their people but also tap into the extraordinary resource that our humanity is.

The Future Is Human

When we develop this holistic perspective on how we function better together as human beings, rethinking performance and how we create results from an understanding of the human connection and how powerful that is, then we can harness our human advantage for ourselves and also for each other. This is why care-driven organizations are asking the questions: "What defines a well-being culture?" and "How do we not only build it but also how do we keep cultivating it?"

A well-being culture is about the quality of our human relationships. The need for community as part of how we thrive has become clear during COVID. Our modern lifestyles have created a lot of lonely people. It's been the conversation I have had with clients through the years, and during the pandemic, it surfaced even more. We see it in suicide attempts where people have lost the connection to life and what matters to them. They no longer feel cared about. I know from my mother's struggle with depression that the loneliness and feeling like she didn't belong or mattered were triggering her deep sense that no one cared about her.

The power of WE is the shared care where we are part of a community and care *about* each other, not just *for* each other. That's why culture has a new job. It's no longer about spaces and places; it's about the conversations that help us feel safe, included, and that we matter. And we are not just talking about creating a safe haven here; we are talking about recognizing what we need so that we can grow. That's why self-care is not the goal; it's how we reach our goals, together.

Social-Emotional Awareness in Our Hybrid World

Essentially, everything is about relationships because everything is an interaction. The people around us affect us, the spaces we are in, and the energy of the group with which we are engaging. We know how it feels to share the pain of the world around us, and equally, we know how it feels to celebrate something together. In addition, we also know the power of sharing ideas and feeling the excitement rise as we build on each other's thoughts.

But what about our new world work environment where some are working fully remotely, in the office full-time, or a mix of the two? Something gets lost when we're not in the same room together. We can all relate to the feeling of experiencing a great moment in virtual meetings where we cheer each other on, only to close down our computer once the meeting is over and look around to realize we're alone. We can also relate to realizing we're on mute when we want to chime in, experiencing multiple people trying to speak at the same time, or seeing many people frustrated that they can't contribute as one person is hogging the airtime.

People who are introverts or deal with social anxiety have loved the isolation of the pandemic while others have hated it. And then there are people like me who have both loved the quiet of deep work that I could do at home and the convenience of not racing from meeting room to meeting room while also deeply missing the feeling of connection that happens when we meet, cheer, share a cup of tea, and even hug. But that's the thing, right? We each interact and engage differently. We have different preferences and needs, and we each read and react differently to the cues that happen when we are together and that we desperately try to understand in a virtual meeting.

That's our social-emotional awareness in action.

I can tell you that as a speaker, I have spoken to thousands of people at a time that I could not see, nor know how they were receiving my words. I didn't know if they were crying or smiling, or even if they laughed. I speak to a little green light on top of my computer telling me I'm connected. I imagine the people on the other side of the screen are like the people I have met in meetings, at conferences, and in office halls who all want the same thing: a better life, a better workplace, and to achieve something in their lives that makes them happy and proud. But speaking virtually is not the same as seeing people's faces when we are together in person. Even if I'm on the stage, we are still connecting through the energy in the room, face to face, and heart to heart.

As we are facing the future of work, where more people work remotely and our gatherings are either virtual or hybrid, the more the opportunities matter when we do meet face to face. The design of meeting spaces and the workplace need to change to facilitate the human connection, be it one on one or in both large and small groups. It's an exciting challenge. But the big question becomes how do we sustain and grow the social-emotional connection that's crucial for both our health, sense of belonging, creativity, and productivity?

Connecting in a Virtual World

To cultivate the kind of culture where we connect on a human level that matters to our well-being and fosters the kind of community that helps us thrive, we have to ask more questions, listen, and make space and time to pause together. If you ask me, it's the only way.

Maybe we begin meetings by pausing together so we all land in the meeting together. To take a moment and really look at each other and notice our own breath so that we can be present and bring our full attention and care to each other.

We must also learn to ask for a pause when something rubs us the wrong way. To throw up a hand and say, "Hey, can we just pause on this for a moment? I want to understand what you mean by that. Can you maybe rephrase what you just said from a perspective of how it might affect all of us and help us solve the problem and achieve the goal we are here to focus on?"

It's just an example of how we can speak up and ask to pause to ensure that we nourish the social-emotional awareness that's crucial for our culture and how we can make self-care the foundation for how we work better together.

To Care Is Our Human Advantage

My first job out of business school was at Royal Copenhagen, a porcelain tableware manufacturer in Denmark. When I arrived to begin my career in the marketing department, they told me that during my first five weeks on the job, I would be at their warehouse to learn what happens from sales to delivery to our customers, and eventually, the end consumer. I was distraught. "At the warehouse?!" I thought to myself. "I have a marketing degree. I am supposed to do marketing work."

Yes, I was young, judgy, ambitious, and thought I was better than that. My aim was high, and I wanted to get on a career track to the top right away, not wasting five weeks at the warehouse. But my frustration didn't last long as I quickly realized the value in understanding the process of the work happening there and meeting the people behind it. I learned a lot of valuable lessons during that time, and in the end, I loved my time there. Later in my career, those lessons also came in handy when I put teams together and set up work processes and workflow because

I knew the value of respecting and having empathy for people and their work-style, asking people for their input, and being an inclusive leader.

Looking back at that time, I now understand what was so special about it and why I enjoyed the work: my fellow teammates. They showed me that having each other's back was vital for everyone to do their best work. It showed me that performance is about interpersonal relationships, and I took that with me.

Everyone was a high performer within the realm of the job that they were expected to do. They had the skills, paid attention, and got it done. But there was one massive factor in how smoothly the teams worked together: They cared about each other. The "What do you need so that you can get your job done AND can I help?" was always the glue that tied the team together. It showed up because we had a bond that said, "I care about you." It was not just in the work though; it was also in the conversations and the laughter during lunch and coffee breaks, which are undeniably the signs of a healthy culture. We talked about family, hobbies, sports, and other things we cared about during these breaks. Sharing what we care about is how we build a healthy culture where we belong, feel respected, safe, seen, and that we matter. We do that together, not alone.

What worked then, works now. It's not that we need fancy new tools to cultivate a strong culture; we need to understand the power of the human connection.

Are we ready to listen and engage with CARE: curiosity, acknowledgement, respect, and empathy?

PAUSE ON THIS

- What are situations that make you feel less included, that you matter, and belong? What are the situations where you feel most included, that you matter, and belong? How do you react or respond differently in either situation?

  _____

  _____

- What kind of conversation, environment, and feedback do you need to feel supported and grow?

  _____

  _____

- How do you feel most encouraged to find your way forward?

  _____

  _____

CHAPTER 17

The Future Is About Work-Life Quality

"Self-care is not a side-hustle."

I was leading a session on Care-Driven Leadership® and discussing how to prevent burnout and foster a well-being culture, when a woman in attendance spoke up. "I have always pursued excellence but I look at the young people today and I see them take lunch breaks and separate their work time from their private time. Listening to you though, I realize that maybe I had it all wrong, thinking excellence is about working non-stop."

I acknowledged that she, like so many others, had learned that giving 100 percent to work and nothing to herself was for a long time how pursuing excellence was viewed. That pursuit of excellence is about work, not people, and results are all that matter, not how we achieve them. We hear entrepreneurs talking about hustling to succeed but most of them burn out before they ever actually do. We are faced with the accepted impression that a high-performance culture is a hustle culture that's highly competitive and not inclusive. However, that's not sustainable, it never was, and at this point, I hope you are recognizing that what truly drives performance and excellence is well-being and care.

Looking at the statistics of what causes burnout, it's clear that it isn't rooted in working too much; it's the loss of agency we experience and worrying too much. It's why the Self-Care Mindset® is so important in cultivating work-life quality.

Yes, we need a balance between the time we spend on work and our private lives. But that's not the answer to solving the burnout crisis. As we've discussed in this book, since our three core relationships (with ourselves, each other, and work) are always connected, we don't stop thinking of work just because we are outside of work. That's why, instead, we need to focus on cultivating a healthy culture built on healthy human relationships, starting with the one we have with ourselves.

You can take as much time off as you want, but if you don't stop worrying, you will still burn out. If you still feel you do not belong and you don't matter, you will still burn out. If you don't feel valued and that you have agency in your own work, you will still burn out. It's not just about cutting out sending emails at night or taking weekends off. That's where you feed and fuel your spirit, but it's not how you prevent burnout.

Having the tools to manage stress and anxiety and taking better care of your emotional and mental health is essential. But I ask you to remember that the last step in the CARE framework is about expressing yourself and using empathy to self-empower and reclaim agency. Don't wait for someone else to give it to you. Ask for it.

Of course, we need to not only talk about making work *work* better for us to be whole humans, but we also need to spark joy by spending time with friends and family. For many, their spiritual life is an important part of cultivating a quality of life. That said, the important trend that will carry into every part of work and life is that we no longer leave our hearts behind. We bring them with us into the work environment because CARE is the new currency that drives not just joy at home, but also joy at work.

Belonging at Work

Gen Z is the next generation that will impact culture and already is doing so. Millennials have been left with the burden of perfection, self-comparison, performance being about more, and putting on the facade that they are okay no matter what, to show they are successful and have their lives together. For the last several years, they are the ones who have burned out the most and the fastest, and not just during COVID, but even before. They inherited expectations and promises that were riddled with the mindset that hard work means achieving success and having the answer means being respected and having status. Growth was about titles and more money. This is the generation that has said, "STOP!" during COVID and asked, "Isn't there more to life than this?" This has played a big part in the Great Resignation, as the masses are saying, "We are no longer willing to just work, work, and work some more, and we want to work in a culture that's respectful and care-driven, valuing us as human beings and listening to our input."

A toxic culture is the number one reason people leave, which means it's not only about people, but it's also about management. As we are changing our relationship with work, we want to belong and matter, and we also want our work to matter and reflect who we are. And more than that, we want well-being to be part of work.

A recent study from Deloitte showed that nearly 70 percent of the C-suite are rethinking work and life and are seriously considering leaving for a job that better supports their well-being. Gen Z wants to work for a company that cares about what they care about. They are focused on social justice and environmental issues and they want to know their voices are heard and matter. Agency is a must and as tech natives, they want the freedom to not only work where and when they want, but they also want to know that they have creative freedom to contribute. The key word is CARE.

Microsoft CEO Satya Nadella has been quoted as saying, "Care is the new currency" and many companies have made it their focus to learn how to cultivate a Culture of Care®. I applaud that, of course, since this has been my focus for several years. However, I want to point out that it's not just about more perks and programs; it took the pandemic for us to open our eyes to the misleading messages about work-life balance as the way to prevent burnout. Time off is not the cure, we need to be driven by something we care about, we need to feel cared about, and we need to cultivate better conversations that come from care. We need Care-Driven Leadership® and we need to stop accepting toxic cultures where people are not respected.

When we care about our work, the risk of burnout is less, and when we are cared about at work, the risk reduces even further. We still need time off, but we should not be using that time to recover from work—that's a sign of a burnout culture. The point here is to understand that what we CARE ABOUT drives us as human beings and what drives culture is that we don't just feel cared for, but also feel CARED ABOUT.

Several companies are encouraging their people to get involved in projects, volunteer work, and community activities during company time because they know that feeding the soul is good for maintaining our humanity, creativity, and connection to ourselves and each other. Some companies increased their well-being and mental health programs during the pandemic but according to studies among employees, many of them are now cutting down on the support. Not only is that too soon, but it will also render them less able to sustain success in the future of work, where well-being is a key strategy for growth.

It's well known that the pandemic has had a negative impact on our collective mental and physical health. Well-being may now be at an all-time low among both the C-suite and rank-and-file employees. According to a study performed by Deloitte, "More than three-quarters of the C-suite

(76 percent) said that the pandemic has negatively affected their well-being, and fewer than two out of three employees rated various dimensions of their health as "excellent" or "good." A new study by Mercer says that 8 in 10 employees are at risk of burnout this year and that thriving employees are seven times more likely to work for a company that prioritizes employee well-being.

I think we can all agree that we want work to be part of our lives and not something that stops us from living with joy or robbing our health but rather work being a place that supports us being healthy and increases our joy.

Work with Heart

Claude Silver is the Chief Heart Officer of VaynerMedia and speaks about the importance of cultivating Emotional Optimism as the most effective tool in revealing the greatness that resides within people. She encourages leaders to lead with the heart and people to integrate heart into their professional lives to become the best version of themselves. Claude also talks about how we need heart-centered leadership to develop elite performance, create cultures of belonging, empower teams to be purpose-driven, efficient, and strong, and infuse companies with empathy, humanity, and joy.

For an organization that has always been known for its hustle culture, it might seem a departure of the brand, but it's the opposite. Gary Vaynerchuck, VaynerMedia CEO, is driven by care and passion, not fear. It's fear that burns us out, not the number of hours we work and so it's a key shift in understanding what drives us. This also gives us some insight into why so many people have become entrepreneurs or pursued side-hustles during the pandemic. We don't want to go to work and leave our hearts behind. We want work to inspire us to live more full and rich lives. We want work to be a place where we grow.

I have worked with many healthcare and front-line workers since the pandemic started, and they are burning out faster than anyone. It's not a secret they are working more hours than ever. But the reason they stay and keep showing up is because they care. However, the other side of care is to worry. You see this with people in the industry of "looking for trouble" as I call it—for example, lawyers, accountants, regulatory type jobs, and controllers. They always have to look for what's out of order, their job is to worry about what might happen. Leaders worry about both their people and the business. Learning to work with our worries in a way that's constructive is how we can reclaim agency and focus on work-life quality instead of needing to get away from work to calm our nerves.

Of course, not everyone can love their work. But it's important to consider they might be driven by love, nonetheless. A parent might choose a job that doesn't inspire them, but it gives them the money and the time to be with their child and support their growth. It's a privilege to be able to focus on work that fulfills us; however, bringing our heart with us to work makes work more fulfilling. It took me years to get to this place, and the effort it took for me to get here was all part of the journey of discovering what I care about. Today, work doesn't feel like work; it feels like it's part of who I am and how I keep growing.

Growth by Choice

Change often happens *to* us at first, and then *for* us. If you look back over your life, you might see that what grew you the most was more often accidental as opposed to choices you made that worked out. Cultivating work-life quality is not just about getting what we want and having a perfect life. It's about consciously making choices along the way so we are more intentional about how we achieve our goals. Not by force and determination, but rather by listening and navigating *what is*.

When I ask people what growth looks like for them, it's often co-dependent on environmental factors such as promotions and opportunities, rather than choices we make to explore, discover, and learn about ourselves. Of course, that's one of the reasons I wrote this book. To keep learning, staying curious, and continuing to grow have been priceless for me and still are.

I hope we never stop learning; I hope we never get to a point where we think we know it all. All growth is chaotic and often why we shy away from it; that messy middle of transitioning between what we know and what we don't know is uncomfortable and uncertain. Should that stop us? Should that keep us from saying, "This is what I want to pursue, what do I need so that I can do that?" Maybe we will get there, maybe not. Maybe we will change our minds along the way. The point is to try and learn along the way rather than thinking we have failed just because it doesn't turn out the way we want.

As we are looking toward the future, let's keep going forward instead of going back to what's familiar, because we know that's not working for us either. Change and growth are a given in life. We can either struggle to change or choose to grow. We can keep asking what we need so that we can face the next step and the next step and the next step. Self-care, well-being, and work-life quality are not destinations; they are a process of living life intentionally and working mindfully.

That's why work-life quality is more than navigating time, taking breaks, and having more time off. It's about cultivating a healthy culture built on healthy human relationships, a culture that's inclusive of our diverse human needs, where we feel safe, that we belong, and that we matter.

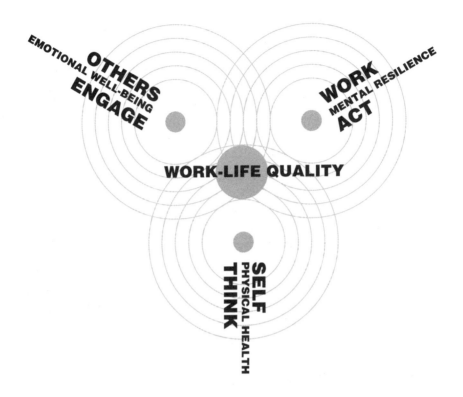

Deconstruct to Build Better

Life is made up of many little steps. So is change. There's a lot we have to unlearn and deconstruct to rethink, create, and build a better work-life quality for ourselves. We have explored the mindset that keeps us stuck, the patterns, habits, and behaviors that we fall automatically into under stress. We have discussed how you can engage in cultivating better conversations with yourself and others and to clear your mind and ask for what you need, so that you can make better decisions. Now, I ask you to pause for a bit longer and spend some time looking at the building blocks and the elements in your life that you need to let go of and unlearn to truly harness the life you want to build.

Working with clients over the years, it was easy to have good intentions but not so easy to learn new habits. The challenge is always to sustain change under pressure. There's a saying in the military that under stress we fall back on our training. If your training is to abandon yourself when times get tough, you will continue to do so. Start training The Self-Care Mindset® now and every day going forward so that when you need care the most, it's there for you. Let self-care be the new training that sustains your life, your health and well-being, and all your relationships.

In his book, *Think Again*, organizational psychologist Adam Grant explores the power of unlearning and rethinking to change our minds. How we invest so much in holding on to what we know that we lose the possibilities that come from keeping an open mind and letting go of what we believe and the convictions that have shaped our lives, but no longer serve us.

To know might be thought of as power. But to know what we don't know is wisdom. For the future of work to be a culture where humans do better, we need to harness change by becoming comfortable with not knowing.

"What Do You Need So You Can Cultivate Work-Life Quality?

There's a great tool that has been used for as long as I can remember by coaches to help people hone in on how they build a life that matters to them; a life that includes what they care about and points to the areas of growth that need to be pursued with intention and care to make it happen. It's called the "Wheel of Life." You can use it to narrow down the details of a specific aspect of growth and you can use it to look at the growth areas in your life as a whole. I like to use it first as a way to take the holistic 360° perspective of what I want my life to consist of and then go into the details of what the daily points of attention are.

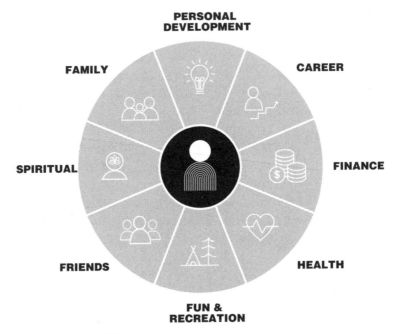

Source: Path For Life®

By doing this exercise, you see where you are out of balance, where you need to pay more attention, and where you are doing well. You can think of it as a way to note where you need to put more energy and where you are overdoing it and putting too much emphasis on something. The Wheel of Life can help you discover parts of a whole life that you might have put on hold and ask yourself if that's what best serves you and your goals. Remember throughout the exercise that we are going to approach it from the perspective that well-being is not the goal itself but rather how we reach our goals. I suggest you create a Wheel of Life for yourself to explore and evaluate how your well-being is feeling for you.

The holistic view can be explored as:

- work and career/professional growth

- personal growth

- family and friends

- health and well-being

- financial well-being

- fun and relaxation

- home

- relationships

You can then take these areas and make a wheel about each one to get to know what you need in even more detail. For example, if you're looking to dive into your personal growth, you may include aspects like:

- spiritual

- reading/studying

- emotional/mental health

- physical health

- social

- boundaries

- positive mindset

- fun

- volunteer work/activism

Along the same lines, if your goal is professional growth, you can break down the aspects like this:

- clarity of communication

- public speaking

- mentors

- skills development

- self-confidence

- accountability

- responsibility

- initiative

- follow-through

You can even tailor Deepak Chopra's seven pillars of well-being for your wheel, which are as follows: 7 to 8 hours of restful sleep, emotional regulation/emotional resilience, meditation and stress management, movement, relationships, nutrition, and laughter.

You can also create your wheel for each of the relationships you have with people at work to explore which are working for you and which ones you want to cultivate further.

Using the Wheel of Life, you can keep exploring what you need personally and professionally to cultivate a life you love, harness your well-being, and reclaim agency over your work-life quality. I suggest that you do this on a regular basis to see how you change and grow and I encourage you to not wait because your best self can't. We all deserve well-being, don't we?

Falling in Love with You

I'm sure you would agree with me that you'd tell the people you care about to stand up for themselves, and encourage them to reclaim their life. You'd want them to see how awesome they are, wouldn't you? You would tell them that it's not how hard they work that makes them great, it's who they are that makes them great. You would encourage them to change their relationship with time so that they would have more fun and not just work. I'm sure you would even tell them that they need to take a lunch-break so they have the energy for what they have to do all afternoon.

I'm sure you'd also tell them they are worthy of care, to stop being so critical of themselves and instead use their self-talk to boost their own self-worth. I'm sure you would want them to cheer themselves on as you cheer for them.

I'm sure you would ask them with compassion and curiosity how they are feeling inside. You would care that they are feeling safe and connected with themselves and can see their way through anxiety.

I'm sure you would ask them questions about what they need to navigate the FUD and I'm also sure you would tell them it's okay to feel stressed and worried. Instead of being stuck going over and over the mistakes they made and what's not working, I'm sure you would want them to focus on what they are working to achieve, why it matters to them, and you would ask them what they need to get there.

I'm sure you would tell them that they can only change and harness what they take responsibility for and support them in coming to terms with *what is*. I'm also very sure you would encourage them to speak up for what they need.

I'm sure you would cheer them on to fall in love with themselves because you can see just how awesome they are, especially when they let their humanity shine through.

You would, wouldn't you?

I ask you to do the same for yourself because you are awesome too. Just being human already makes you amazing and having the opportunity to be you is the cherry on top.

You can't wait. You deserve self-care every day too.

PAUSE ON THIS

- What do you want your work and life to include?

  _____

  _____

- How do you want to grow and what do you need to let go of to do so?

  _____

  _____

- What can you change for now to take the small steps that add up to change?

  _____

  _____

- Who are your cheerleaders and supporters going to be along the way?

  _____

  _____

CHAPTER 18

A Culture of CARE®

"People who pause together, care better and create impact together"

Seth Godin is an author, changemaker, and thought-leader. I think of his brilliance as his ability to pause, listen, and ask questions to hone in on what's really going on to understand the consumer; how they think, feel, and make choices. I have followed Seth for years, and I've been a part of his community-driven projects, like his altMBA, and most recently, *The Carbon Almanac*, which is a book that gives people who care about the environment the facts to take action by making discerning choices about our carbon impact.

He believes that when people work together, we harness ideas, inspire change, and make a difference. He's right because when we mutually care about something, we can create change, growth, and impact. I have learned three questions from Seth that I always use to avoid falling into the trap of doing more—and instead—pause to do better:

- "What's it for?"

- "Who's it for?"

- "Why does it matter?"

I asked these questions when I started this book. I ask them when I discuss new ideas with my team. And I ask them when someone feels a bit lost about the decisions they have to make.

Seth looks at our human behavior as driven by these five factors: fear, being overwhelmed, which leads to our desire for ease, greed that's fueled by survival fear, curiosity, and generosity stemming from connection. He talks about the tension we feel when facing change and the need to learn to embrace it to avoid getting stuck.

In a similar way, you can see how The Self-Care Mindset® brings you through your own behaviors based on FUD, pausing to get curious, and then reclaiming your choices with care and mindfulness. The heart of the matter for our humanity to thrive is connection and generosity. Can we wake up every day and challenge ourselves to stay present and make choices that matter, not just for ourselves, but also for each other and the people we serve?

Care Reaches All the Way to Your Customer

Companies, salespeople, advisors, lawyers (any position that is customer service and client connected) tend to have a mindset that the customer is at the center of the business model. This means that everything is about the customer and they come first. When we work in the service of our clients, we tend to put their needs above all, prioritizing to solve their demands, and abandoning ourselves in the process, rather than realizing that how we care about ourselves impacts how we care, connect, and communicate.

Speaking with people in these positions, it's clear they are burning out and sometimes even frazzled by the never-ending need to be available to solve their client's problems.

I encourage them to pause and ask, "What do I need so that I can best solve my client's needs?"

That's how a Culture of Care® reaches all the way to the customer.

If you're anything like me, you don't want someone to be available to you, you want someone to be present with you. You want someone to truly listen to your concerns, understand what good would look like for you, and care about what you care about. You don't want someone to just give you what you want; you want them to ask better questions to find out how they can truly help you to get what you actually need.

Using The Self-Care Mindset® to reach all the way to our customers, we create a culture that is care-driven instead of just customer-driven.

Moments of Presence

We can use Power-Pausing with anyone and everyone to create better moments of connection leading to better relationships and trust. We can pause together. We can pause as a team. We can pause before we respond. And we can pause just because we need a moment of presence to reconnect with what we care about and why it matters.

Well-being means different things to each of us and the respect and care that comes from pausing and listening to each other allows for that to emerge. Leaders often ask me how they can inspire their teams to self-care without overstepping boundaries. My response is always the same, by doing it yourself. Pause more. Show your people that you pause. Pause with them. Be curious for just a little longer. Ask more questions. And know that it's okay to ask someone how they are doing, but it's not okay to assume, judge, or to tell them what you think they need and pressure them to share with you.

Many people are still concerned about privacy and autonomy when it comes to health and well-being at work. But you can still say, "I'm here if you want to talk." And say it because you mean it and are able to be present to someone. They will know if you are authentic because you show that you know what it's like to be human too. Because you truly care about their well-being, because just like them, you know what it's like to hide and pretend you are okay, even when you are not. Because you too know that it hurts when we think that we just have to be resilient and push through instead of pausing to be mindful about what we need to feel we matter, be whole humans, and work better because of it. The point is to care. Caring about yourself, others, and the work you do is how we find a way forward together.

As a leader, you show you care when you pause, listen, and ask questions about what your people need to solve what's facing them, and give them the space and time to answer. This is not supposed to be rapid-fire. Let them reclaim their agency, be it for their emotional and mental well-being or a project where they are stuck and you can support them using the AAA tool and asking better questions.

Grief at Work

Loss comes to us all at some point in our lives. Loss is isolating and we tend to grieve alone. However, as we are rethinking culture and how we care better together at work, grief is a conversation we need to include. The difficult conversations are often the most transformative and the ones that cultivate the trust and psychological safety that we need to foster a healthy work culture.

The challenge is that grief is personal and each of us grieves differently. Some want to talk about it, some don't, others simply don't know how to talk about it. The worst of it is that we feel awkward and say something that sounds like a greeting card or something downright hurtful like, "You will get over it, don't worry."

When I lost my parents, I didn't want to get over it; I wanted to learn to live with it. I didn't fit into the "normal" grief groups, where people were asking why it happened, because I felt it was more tormenting to ask questions that we could never answer. The meaning of life is a question we tend to seek the answer to for our entire life and if we keep asking it until the end, it can become a curious way of living and learning. However, the meaning of death is not one I think we can learn to understand. To me, it became about learning to accept, not understand.

I was fired after my mom died and it seemed no one knew how to talk about grief so getting rid of the problem was the best way to go, for them. Of course, that was not the official reason. Some need to get back to work to get their mind on something that brings about a sense of normalcy, not able to be at home, where the void is big and dark. Some need time to process because the emotions are constantly triggered. That's what happened to me after my first divorce, I was taken aback and stunned, and I simply couldn't shake the feeling of betrayal. I sat in my office cubicle crying through the day, and I was thankful that my job didn't expect much of me.

Loss has been a constant part of my life story and it's part of my resilience too. However, my resilience has changed. It now comes from being transparent about what I'm feeling and asking people to simply listen to me talk, without giving me advice about how to fix it. I ask them if they are okay to just hold space for me, and I have a few friends who are great at that.

How do we hold that space in the workplace? We have teams that perhaps want to grieve together, between having lost team members to COVID, mass shootings, and war. This is something we neither can nor should ignore. I believe that we need to give people the care and respect to ask them what they need, and for each of us to answer that, we need to ask that of ourselves first.

Leaders ask how to best have the conversations with their team members and how they can ask people how they are doing without overreaching. My answer: ask them. Let's stop assuming we know what people want and need. The reality is that we each need to deal with our own discomfort of talking about grief before we can be present with someone else's grief. We do this by simply holding space and letting them speak, without "me-too-ing," interruptions, and "good advice" about how to deal or get over it. Even when someone says, "I don't know how I'm going to get through this," don't tell them how you think they should act, just listen. Maybe say a kind yes and ask how you can help or what they would need from you, if anything. Leave it up to them to know the right time to ask for help and to figure that out. At first, they are just getting familiar with grief, and they are not ready to "fix it," even if it's painful. Our nervous system needs to adjust to the shock of loss. This goes from being fired, to betrayal, divorce, and the loss of loved ones. I'm not saying the loss is the same, I'm saying grief comes in many shapes.

The shock of loss is life-altering. It's the period of time where we realize that all our hopes and dreams and our expectations about life and the days ahead have just disappeared. Losing my mom suddenly and my dad over a longer period of time, where we had the opportunity to grieve together, I can say that I prefer the latter, even if it was difficult to go through. In both cases, our grief accompanies us to work. Even if we use work to distract ourselves, our emotions don't stay at home, they stay with us and in us.

If you are grieving, please ask for the support and care that you want, be it space and time, a hug, or sharing a cup of tea to talk about your loss. People ask me if it hurts to talk about my parents and if I would prefer not to. It's a great question because it gives me the opportunity to share how much I love talking about my parents because it reminds me of the love that lives on. Whatever you need, please don't think you have to go at it alone and please also know when you need to be alone.

I don't believe we get over it, we learn how to live with it and as much as we need support to get through it, we also need to go at our own pace. Loss is like going numb and being frozen. When we can start to open back up to receive the love from the memories we carry with us, we begin to feel the circulation of love again. As my dad said right before he passed, "All we have in the end is love." What is so clear to me is how much love and grief go hand in hand.

For the future of work to be more human, we need to respect and care about all the things that make us human. Our humanity is a gift to embrace and harness, together.

Care Matters

It's easy to lose sight of the bigger picture when the daily stuff needs to be taken care of and busy is the new normal. I invite you to get clear about what you care about, the big strokes and the small ones because even under pressure, care is the strongest and most resilient emotion that drives us. It keeps us aligned with our ethics, hopes, and dreams. We often hear that love is the strongest emotion but I believe care is. Care is universal. You can care about the environment and feel strongly that we need to make daily choices that protect our resources. You might love the view, the animals, the fields, the ocean, and the mountains. It's your personal experience that makes you feel the love, whereas CARE is shared.

We become activists because we care. We show up because we care. We speak up because we care. And we choose the company we want to work for, and the people we enjoy working with, because we care about the same things. That's how we create change and impact together.

The future of work is about CARE. On every level, care is the mindset that keeps us focused on what matters, including our well-being. Care is what takes us out of the survival mode of fear, greed, and cutting corners to get by. It's how we are able to face the FUD and stay curious and courageous. It's how we can connect, communicate, and collaborate with kindness and generosity and make choices that regenerate our daily energy, focus, and attention so that we can keep building a strong, healthy, and sustainable Culture of Care® together. One that doesn't burn out from worry but rather builds on our strengths, harnessing our human advantage to care.

It's the kind of leadership that doesn't focus on what's not working but rather catches people in what they are doing right, building on our strengths, and being curious about what we can add to the conversation by being more inclusive of our diverse human skills, talents, and ways of thinking.

It's the kind of culture where we stop running on survival mode, driven by fear, and instead are inspired by what we care about. Where performance is about pausing to solve the right problem and pursuing growth by asking questions. It's the work environment where people feel they want to work because it feeds who they are and fuels their growth.

We can all choose to change the way we work; however, we work better together when we recognize that our humanity is not a problem to solve but rather an advantage to harness. When self-care is no longer a personal problem but instead a work-culture possibility.

What Will You Choose?

Going back to where the seed was planted in 1999, little did I know it would become the year my parents got cancer just a few months after I had divorced for the second time and changed jobs. They say don't change too much all at once, and it certainly wasn't what I had planned. But that time and the experiences in my life changed me forever and allowed me to keep growing today. I have come to understand that even though change and growth are scary or uncomfortable, it's essential to life. We need self-care to harness change and grow so that our well-being is the foundation for achieving our goals. We must stop fear from running our lives and we must stop working on survival-mode. Instead, let's pause more to protect and harness our most important resource—our humanity.

Care Is What Motivates Us, Not Fear

Scuba-diving on a beautiful day at the Needles Eye by Darwin's Island, I was excited as the day before we'd dropped down right in the middle of a migration of hammerhead sharks. It was a magical experience. Awe-inspiring. As far as I could see, above me and below me, these amazing and graceful animals were just passing by us for 20 minutes straight.

So there we were, about to drop straight down into 35 feet of water to avoid the current and make it across the abyss to the diving area for the day. Being a dive master, I went last, holding on to my camera, ready to be one with the ocean and her treasures. But just mere moments after being in the water, I got thrown off course and felt like I was in a washing machine. As I tumbled around, my regulator, which allows divers to breathe under water, was ripped out of my mouth.

When I finally got my bearings, I looked at my depth gauge and realized I was in 15 feet of water, not 35 feet of water. "How did I end up here?" "What's going on?"

I needed air. I couldn't go to the surface as we'd been warned to avoid doing that at all costs because the current would slam us into the rocks of the Needles Eye. I was fighting against the current and the undertow, trying to stay down in the water as close to the sandy bottom as possible, crawling toward the depths of the ocean, reaching for my regulator so I could breathe again.

Still holding my breath, trying to stop myself from tumbling, I realized in that moment I had two choices. I could either take a breath of water and my life would be over. Or I could fight.

It may sound cliché, but it was as if my life flashed before my eyes. I thought of my parents as they were still alive at the time, and I knew my death would devastate them.

In case you are wondering, I decided to fight for my life.

I got my regulator back into my mouth, and I started screaming into it while choking, drawing in as much breath as possible, hyperventilating at this point, and crawling into the ocean's depth against the current. I finally made it down to 35 feet of water, crossed the abyss, and joined the rest of the team. Shaking, I grabbed onto one of the arms of the guide, and I did not let go till we finished the dive and got back on the boats.

I realized later that I was not screaming out of fear of losing my life; I was screaming because I wanted my life—I wanted to live.

That's how I was able to harness such immense focus, energy, and power to keep fighting against the fear, and the current. I was fighting for my life because I cared about the people who cared about me.

Fear is not a sustainable motivator; care is. It's what we care about that keeps us motivated. It's what we care about that gives us strength and focus. It's what we care about together that makes a difference in our own lives and in the lives of the people we serve, and it's how we create the change we want to see in the world. The actions and choices we make all add up to sustainable change and growth. Because we care.

Self-Care Is a Conversation; Let's Keep it Going

I hope that we can all learn to communicate from a place of care by being aware and inclusive of our own needs, respecting each other, and speaking from a place of healthy boundaries that focuses on how we build a Culture of Care® together.

A culture where we can be who we are because we feel safe, belong, and matter.

A culture where care is the foundation for how we do our best work together.

A culture where *people first* means that we care *about* people, not just *for* people.

A culture where we feel we have worth, bring value, and can raise our hand and ask for help without fearing we will be viewed as incapable or unable.

A culture where we can embrace mental health as something we all have and need to care for together by saying no to working in survival mode and instead cultivating the common practice of Power-Pausing.

A culture where The Self-Care Mindset® is a new language we all share so that we can be fully self-expressed.

A care-driven culture that holds space for care-driven conversations.

Care Makes Us Stronger Together

I invite you to care more, not less. Care matters. When we care together, we make a difference, we inspire each other, we change and grow together. People who care together, create impact together. Care is the new currency that will change the way we work and live, for good.

Let's build self-care into our daily lives. Let's care about each other. And let's share the care to create the kind of future where human beings belong and work better together.

I hope you will share with others what you have learned here. When we share what we learn, we grow, and we inspire others to do the same. It's how we cultivate a Culture of Care® where everyone gets the tools to navigate their whole human well-being.

"May all beings be happy. May all beings be healthy. May all beings be free of suffering. May all beings live in peace. May all beings know that they matter and make a difference in the world, and may all beings learn to live and work with care, together."—Buddhist prayer.

May the PAUSE be with you.

ABOUT THE AUTHOR

Jeanette Bronée is a culture strategist, global keynote and TEDx speaker, and the CEO and founder of Path For Life®, Inc. She is an internationally recognized well-being expert who is rethinking self-care in the workplace as the foundation for peak performance, engagement, and a culture where people belong and work better together.

Integrating her 20 years of business experience in marketing, retail management, and team development with her background in mindfulness, health, and well-being, Jeanette has developed the CARE-driven framework. She shows us how to shift from a burnout mindset, operating in survival mode, to a Self-Care Mindset®, where we can harness our human advantage and create a Culture of Care®. Jeanette provides tools so that we can reclaim agency over our work and lives by understanding our mindset and taking charge of our well-being as the foundation for personal and professional growth. She also shows how we can cultivate the human connection that helps us communicate and collaborate with curiosity and care so that we can navigate challenges and thrive in our constantly changing reality.

Jeanette has spoken at the United Nations and in countries across five continents about how we can facilitate change in our relationship with resilience, mental health, and well-being at work so that we can be busy *and* healthy at the same time, cultivating a culture where together we can create impact, growth, and sustainable success.

Index